Un-Perfect

A not-so-graceful journey into motherhood

By Kelly Nordstrom

© 2010 Kelly Nordstrom

All rights reserved. Copyright under Berne Copyright
Conventions, Universal Copyright Convention and Pan-
American Copyright Convention. No part of this book may
be reproduced, stored in a retrieval system or transmitted in
any form, or by any means, electronic, mechanical,
photocopying, recording or otherwise, without prior
permission of the publisher.

11 10 09 08 07   6 5 4 3 2

Published by Indigo Heart Publishing
200 East Rainbow Ridge Circle, The Woodlands, Texas
77381

Cover Design by Gary Bazman

ISBN-13: 978-0-9827803-0-5

Dedicated to my
beautiful daughters
Parker and Paige,
Two
giggly
amazing
bright lights shining
in this big 'ol universe.

Contents

Prologue...i

Open Letter to My Daughter...................vii

LIFE CHAPTER 1: Ignorant Bliss............1

LIFE CHAPTER 2: Confusion..............125

LIFE CHAPTER 3: Healing.................209

EPILOGUE....................................299

RESOURCES.............................311

Prologue

June 15, 1956:
A child's life is a blank sheet of paper upon which each parent
writes.

~ Violet King, my grandmother

I found this entry in my grandmother's journal when she passed away a few years ago. I wish I could say my first year of being a mother was written on my daughter's sheet with grace and elegance, but it wasn't. I stumbled, fell to the ground, and finally dusted off my knees and held my head high again.

Each day we are writing our own book, whether we realize it or not. Sometimes we close chapters so gently we're not even aware of it until we look back and have to pull up the pages to remember. Sometimes we feel the flutter of pages against our hearts and understand that a chapter is opening. Other times, we firmly slam it shut, vowing never to return.

Life moves and flows, opening and closing just like a book. Each chapter breathes in a beginning, breaks with excitement or pain in the middle, and quietly exhales in the end. It has to happen that way because our own unique book of life breathes with us, expanding and contracting.

This book documents three of my Life Chapters: Ignorant

Bliss, Confusion, and Healing. It is based upon my journal entries during that period of my life. It is tears and frustration. It is laughter and celebration. It is my heart and soul spilled onto paper. Please be gentle. It is my subjective truth.

My husband Derek has his own entries. He was not privy to my secret struggle and his perspective reflects that. We went through the book together and I would ask, "What do you remember about this time in our life?" and I would add his memories of the events. Sometimes I was shocked that he was so unaware of my state of mind. I protected my depression fiercely; so much so that my own husband had no idea I was suicidal.

Our life together now is authentic and real. And good. I love Derek Kayne Nordstrom with all my heart. I tell him all the time, "You are my favorite person in this world. Of all the people in it, you are my favorite." I consider myself incredibly lucky to be married to him. He is my best friend. And we LAUGH. The tears-streaming-down-your-face kind of laugh. The real stuff. The good stuff.

As I write this, it is early 2010. Looking back on my experiences, it feels like a slow descent into insanity and a quick leap out. Some might even say *too* quick - I know it's not what a lot of people experience. Most people hit rock bottom and make slow and steady progress back up. I'm not "most people", I'm just Kelly. And I have my own twisted, special journey that's all mine, which apparently means an abnormally quick "recovery" without medication or therapy.

I literally woke up and decided that I had to start healing RIGHT NOW or I wasn't going to make it. I was at that place: Either die or get better. It was more of a panicky reaction than anything else. I scratched and clawed my way out without looking back. It was like running away from a beast in a forest. I saw glimpses of light through the trees and hauled ass running toward it. I didn't look back to see how close the beast was because even turning around to look at it slowed me down. That's how my "semi-recovery" felt.

I didn't fully recover until 2009, after working with an amazing therapist for more than two years. Until then I coasted, drenched in terror that postpartum OCD, depression and psychosis would come back. I suffered from guilt and worthlessness for all those terrible thoughts and images. When my children and husband told me they loved me, my only thought was this: "If you knew what my mind is capable of, you wouldn't love me."

It took a long time to wrap my head around the fact that I wasn't to blame for my experience. Yes, I housed the sickness in my head and body, but I didn't choose it. Six years after my experience I finally felt safe enough to turn back and face the beast. I could not have done that without a therapist.

Regarding medication... this is a tough subject. Even though I chose not to go on medication, I couldn't possibly encourage anyone else to blindly follow in my footsteps. Some very dear friends and family have seen major improvements in their lives from prescribed medication. Every person is unique and so is their journey. I respect and honor individual choices. I support all people, medication or no medication. 'Nuff said.

Some people that think that postpartum symptoms can be neatly classified as one of three things: Depression, OCD/anxiety or psychosis. I don't think this is true. I believe the experience can be kind of a mudslide from one to the other. For example, my experience started with a truckload of OCD and anxiety, which became so intense I sank into depression with psychotic tendencies, which led to suicidal thinking. They are still separate disorders, just not separate experiences. A person can experience them concurrently.

Disclaimer: I am NOT a psychiatrist. Psychosis is a very serious term and I don't use it lightly. I have never been formally diagnosed, but based on the definition I believe I fit the symptoms.

Psychosis is defined as a "break with reality". Delusions are one hallmark of this illness. Here's why I think I had a break with reality: While my intrusive thoughts terrified me, the thought of me being the devil's daughter did not frighten me one bit. In my mind, it was fact and nothing could have changed that belief. From what I know today, this indicates a delusion, a break from reality, meaning psychosis. However, there are varying degrees of psychosis and as terrifying as my experience was, I think I had a "lite" version of it (if such a thing exists).

I desperately tried to find a reason for the images and thoughts I was experiencing. I was terrified of my own mind and needed to find a reason. My explanation was this: I was the daughter of the devil and had a split personality. I believed those delusions with every fiber in my body and nothing could convince me otherwise. I believed I was adopted and my real parents were demons. I was paranoid that my family knew my secret and talked about it after I left my parent's house. It's so bizarre to even type this, but it is what I believed at the time. My parents could have supplied all the evidence in the world to prove that I was their child, but I'm guessing it would only have pushed me further into the delusion. I would have been paranoid that they were worried about the secret, not about me.

There seemed to be a section of time, about two months (late June of 2001 to mid-August of 2001), where my experience sank into psychosis.

All these labels could invite a fist fight between doctors, psychiatrists, sufferers, and survivors in the postpartum world. Every person will read this book and have their own slight spin on how terms and labels are used. I mean no harm by using medical terms and labels.

It's simply my raw experience and my intent is to share my

story and get into the guts of what it felt like to me to live with, suffer from, and finally conquer, postpartum depression, OCD/anxiety, and psychosis.

Open Letter to My Daughter

March 13, 2010

Hi honey, it's me, Mom. This story is about my entrance into motherhood with you, my first daughter, Parker Sue. Yes, you were severely colicky, but that's not who you are. As I write this, you are a magnificent nine-year-old that giggles, hugs, cares, and loves. Your hugs are tight and your smile is bright. You were not a bad baby, you were a beautiful baby who was in pain. You did not cause my postpartum experience. My postpartum experience was my reaction to an uncontrollable situation.

I had an unrealistic desire to be the perfect mother for you. Little did I know that you would have loved me just the way I am. I know this because as I write this, you're almost ten years old, and my secret is out: I'm human. I make truckloads of mistakes. And you still hug me when you get off the bus from school. I love your hugs.

I wrote this book because there are a lot of women out there who are hurting, and this book can help them feel a little less alone and scared. I hope you can understand that. It was a difficult decision to write about the raw reality of my experience, but every time I tried to soften the details, your dad encouraged me to stay true and honest. He said, "If you go halfway, women are still going to feel alone in their experience." He's right. I couldn't cut corners

vii

on the real experience, as petrifying as it is to publish it.

I also wrote this book because if you choose to have children, you may be a candidate for this twisted journey called postpartum depression (OCD, anxiety, psychosis). I didn't want to cushion the details because if you (or anyone else in this world) experience the raw, terrifying thoughts I did, I didn't want you to feel alone or like you're worse than I was and have you feel hopeless. There is always hope.

I wanted to publish this book and blow the roof off all the secrecy, too. Motherhood is difficult with or without postpartum depression. Unfortunately, the only way I know how to unleash this secret is to write about my experience. This decision ropes you into the public eye without your consent or understanding. You didn't volunteer for a starring role in this book, but I could not write about my experience without including you. I want the world to understand that while a mother can suffer through this condition, she still has the capacity to love her children. I have loved you every single minute of every single day.

By the time you and your sister have children, I hope I've done enough work to have amazing recovery routes ready for you if you need them. And of course, you'll have Dad and me. We know a thing or two about supporting women in an emotionally delicate place. :)

So please know that through this entire experience, my love for you never faltered. You were always the shining beacon at the end of a dark tunnel. As you read some of the pages, it may be difficult to understand that, but it's true. Every single day I loved you more than I could even comprehend. I am so thankful to have you in my life.

I cherish you, love you, treasure you, and admire you. Forever. I love you, Parker Sue.

I'm no poet, but here's how I feel about bringing you into this world:

My **soul** called for you

From across the universe

To bring you here

Into loving manifestation.

You are pure **light** and **joy.**

Thank you for being **you.**

This is my story.

It's not perfectly written

and I could beat myself up for it, but I won't.

Read with a gentle heart and open mind.

Compassion is required.

Please leave ridicule and criticism at the doorstep.

Thank you.

Love,

Kelly

You must be wounded into writing,

But you shouldn't write

Until the wound has healed.

~ Tolstoy

Clueless and Panicked.

I was panicked and overwhelmed, but smiled through it. I would have never, not in a million years, guessed that a year later I would be suicidal.

Kelly Nordstrom

LIFE CHAPTER 1: IGNORANT BLISS

A blessed path is only blessed

if you understand

there's something more out there

that could make it otherwise.

How can you appreciate good

If you've never experienced bad?

Un-Perfect

The Present: March 24, 2010

There is a secret. It makes a lot of mothers feel hopeless, helpless, sad, and guilty. It makes them question their worth and it depletes their confidence. Successful, happy, smart women become confused, overwhelmed, and scared.

Allow me to blow the roof off this secret right now: Motherhood can suck. Bad. I've been there. And when I say I've been there, I mean I have been "rock-bottom-postpartum/OCD/depression/psychosis" kind of there.

Where I've been may fascinate you. It may offend you. It may make you feel like a better mother than me. It may help you feel less alone. It may give you hope.

But to do any of those things for you, we need to start at the beginning in the Past...

May 19, 2000

I just gave birth. I know that doesn't seem extraordinary, but the fact that I did it, makes it extraordinary to me. Me. Just an average run-of-the-mill Minnesota girl who had sex with her husband nine months ago and now here I am with our daughter, Parker Sue. I'm so relieved. For the past month I've been staring at my enormous belly wondering how something that huge was going to fit through a space that was barely large enough for my husband's uh, "hotdog".

Much to my amazement, she did fit... and now here I am sitting in my hospital room with my daughter on the *outside* of my body. And ironically, we're both wearing diapers. Didn't see that coming. Why didn't anyone tell me about the size of this incredible maxi pad? If I taped two of these together, I could wear it as a strapless dress. I find myself more embarrassed about this pad than I did when five people were staring at my crotch during my daughter's magical entrance into life.

I asked the nurse if this baby could exit out of my ass. There goes my dignity. For the entire thirteen hours of labor I was obsessed with thinking my child was going to be the first anal birth. I kept asking the nurse, "Are you sure you've never witnessed an ass birth? Are you positive?" She laughed. Derek laughed. I didn't laugh.

So here we are. She was born through the correct hole and now here we lay together in diapers. Parker Sue was born this morning at 2:49 a.m. She's three hours old. I'm waiting for the clock to strike a reasonable hour so I can call everyone I know on the planet to spread the news that I officially have the cutest baby in the world. She is the sweetest thing I've ever seen in my life. I keep looking at each detail thinking, "These toenails. I made them. Her lips, I made those too. Five fingers and toes. How on earth did my body know how to make these things? How did *she* know how to make all these things?" I'm amazed. I didn't realize I could do such a great job without supervising every detail at every juncture, but here's proof. I actually do a better job when I release control.

I didn't even try to control Derek through the whole labor and delivery ordeal. I just let him do his thing, which unfortunately, was to doubt my birthing skills every step of the way. There's no other way to say it; he was a panicked mess. At one point he was leaning into my face while I was pushing, saying,

Un-Perfect

"There is no way in hell you're getting this kid out, there's just no way, it's not possible, you're going to need a c-section, you can't do this, holy shit, this is insane..." He was the anti-cheerleader. "That hole's too small/you know it's true/that hole's too small/can't get it through/Hey-O, Hey-O, Hey-Hey-O!"

In the haze of excruciating pain, I remember the nurse telling him to shut it. I would have given her a high five if I didn't feel like trolls were chewing on my tailbone. But she had a point: If you don't have anything positive to say, don't say it. Especially when your wife is having your baby.

But in the end, through the panic and rainfall of swear words, I delivered our baby girl. Derek and I laughed and cried and shook our heads in disbelief.

We're actually PARENTS now. A mom and dad. I'm a MOM. I'm someone's mom. "Hi, I'm Parker's mom." I'm a *mother*. Not a mother*fucker*, just a MOTHER. A mom.

May 20, 2000

I shuffled my sore body down the hall to see Parker in the nursery. It took me about 7 hours, but I finally got to the maternity window. Peaceful babies were lined up like little burritos in baskets, except one in the corner screaming her face off.

It was not a good sign when the nurse was relieved to see me. She was pointing to the little hurricane, asking (begging), "Is this one yours?!" She was panicked and she's actually trained in infant care. If she can't handle her, how

4

*am I supposed to take care of her? I couldn't even hold down
a steady babysitting gig when I was a teenager. I should've
attended a Mom Boot camp of some sort.*

I hated babysitting. I'd put the kids to bed at 6:00 p.m. and call my boyfriend over. Then I'd eat all their chips, washing them down with wine coolers. I remember one little girl saying, "But those chips are for my lunch!" I replied, "So? I'm the babysitter." I was such an asshole. I remember threatening one girl with releasing her bird out of its cage if she didn't go to bed. I'm sure her therapist is itching to get a hold of me so I can apologize for that one.

You know that feeling when you are painfully aware of life moving forward and you're not ready? It kicks you in the ass then shoves you through the door to begin a new chapter whether you like it or not. That's where I am. I want to stuff her back inside my belly where she isn't such a hell raiser and I don't feel like such an imbecile.

It's unfortunate to realize this at such an inopportune moment, but I think I have serious commitment issues. I even quit tennis in high school because I wasn't the best one on the team. I'd throw my racket and storm off the court if I didn't win. I was such a whiny baby. But I can't quit motherhood if I'm not the best one on the planet. I can't throw my Baby Bjorn out the car window and drive off into the sunset. This is commitment of the highest order.

Okay Kelly. Get a grip. You're 30 years old, for God's sake. You can do this.

This cannot be as bad as I'm thinking. I'm just panicking and that's totally normal, right? I mean, she's part of me and part of Derek. Big deal. Neither of us are horrible people. She can't be that bad. I grab her flailing arms and legs and in a sweet singsong voice say, "I am not good at this, I cannot do

Un-Perfect

this, I am not good enough for this."

I'm not good enough.

Couldn't I have started with a beginner baby like all the other moms out there? The one that sleeps and huddles into my chest like it knows where it came from. That's the one I need. Not this screaming, sweating, bright red ball. The nurse was droning on and on about taking care of her, but I was too panicked to hear anything.

I'm certain the she said something to the effect of, "I don't get paid enough for this shit".

I'm not getting paid at all.

And I'm pretty sure I'd be fired if it was possible.

May 22, 2000

Okay, we're home. Now what? We stare at her all the time waiting for her to scream for a bottle. This occurs about every two hours. The nurses told us to make her wait four hours and get her on a schedule, but they have no idea what we're dealing with. Other babies cry; our baby goes from zero to sixty in the blink of an eye. If we don't jam a bottle into her face within seconds of starting to fuss, she starts screaming so hard her entire body turns red. She sweats like a triathlete.

We panic every time. I'm usually bouncing her up and down yelling, "Derek! Where is it! Hurry up! No, pour the water in the bottle like THIS, goddamn it, no not like that! I don't care if there are clumps floating in it! Give it to me!"

Derek makes the bottle at such a breakneck speed that formula is all over the counter and on the floor when he's finished. It appears she's bonging her bottle because it's finished in about three minutes flat. I don't even have time to burp her because if I pull her face away from that bottle, she screams bloody murder.

A few times I've tried it because I don't think it's healthy to bong food. So she'll be screaming while I'm patting her back and Derek will yell from the kitchen while cleaning up the bottle disaster, "What are you doing? Put it back in her mouth!" So I do. Then we wait for the spit-up. We've learned to just have towels everywhere in the house for easy clean-up. I'm worried she's not getting any nourishment because it is exploding out of her face. Is this normal? I have no idea.

These hysterical "bottle fire drills" are exhausting. It's like running a race and never crossing the finish line because we have to do it again in two hours (not four as the nurse would suggest). I wish we could've brought home one of those nurses from the maternity ward. They know everything. What makes them think we know what we're doing? Because we read some books? I've never been a parent before. I have no idea how to zip this baby into our lives and fully integrate all three of us into one family. It feels like three separate people in the house instead of one cohesive unit. We're all parts right now instead of a sum.

Parker lives in the vibrating bouncy seat. This morning Derek said, "I don't know about this vibrating thing - how is it different than shaking a baby?

Un-Perfect

Do you think it's causing brain damage?"

Well shit, NOW I do. I'm certain the vibrating bouncy seat is causing brain damage. Of course it is. I've already ruined her and she's only three days old.

I called the nurse line and asked if there is a time limit on the vibrating bouncy seat before it causes brain damage. She said, "Honey, I say if it keeps the baby quiet, then go for it."

I can't be sure, but I thought I heard laughing as she hung up the phone. I know she thinks we're being ridiculous. Whatever. Of all the books, classes, and conversations, none of it prepared us for feeling so inadequate.

May 23, 2000

It's not like this baby thing was a surprise to us - we just don't have a clue. We planned this entry into parenthood as much as we could have planned. I have been with Derek for nine and a half years now, so we know each other inside and out. I know that when he starts scratching at his cuticles he feels overwhelmed. I know he wants to sit in an Irish pub someday drinking Guinness, listening to everyone's accents. He knows that I'll yap everyone's ear off at parties, and then come home to ask for the replay: Did anyone seem annoyed that I talked so much? When I touched that person's shoulder, did they seem awkward? Derek is the Zen to my hype.

Kelly Nordstrom

Anyway, our life has continued on a perfectly straight line of progression: We dated for three years, engaged for a year, married three years, tried getting pregnant for a year, which brings us to now, being married for five years with a newborn daughter. We are Mom and Dad now, instead of Kelly and Derek.

We laid some good foundation. A house in the 'burbs and steady jobs. We talked about having a baby and read truckloads of books and we thought we understood the nuts and bolts of parenting. We were ready and made the mature decision to go off the pill. And then of course we had nine of months of pregnancy to plan even *more*, but we still feel lost in the woods. How can this be? We are intelligent people (at least I thought so).

We just learned her pacifier was built for an 18-month-old. It covers her entire face like a goddamn manhole. I'm worried she'll suffocate on it. We didn't know there were sizes on pacifiers. How did we not know that pacifiers came in sizes? How does everyone on this planet know about these things except us?

That's it. I'm hopping in my car right now to grab the newborn size. Maybe that's why she's so pissed. Her pacifier is too big. Of course that's it. That is why she screams all the time. Once I get the right pacifier, everything will be fine and happy. I'm counting on it, actually. Three days of screaming sucks.

But I've got to be fair, here. I'm a little obnoxious and brash, so why wouldn't my daughter be the same? Let's face it, wherever I am, you'll know I'm there. I'm the one in the back of the bar screaming, "YEAAAAHHH!!!! WWAAAAAOOOHHH!" I'm not drunk, just incredibly loud and having a really, really great time.

I'm the one at the baby shower that, when my friend stands up to make her speech, I whistle at her, because she's still a sexy momma (and because she looks scared to death standing in the spotlight and I want to help ease the pain).

Un-Perfect

If I take a cab somewhere, by the end of the trip I will know: The driver's family, his sleep schedule, his other job, and that he enjoys playing the banjo.

I can make a friend anywhere, anytime. Plus, I think it's important to connect with the driver on a personal level to avoid the chances of a knife being pulled on me.

If I worked with you, you'd know me on your first day. I'd be the one at your cubicle extending a warm welcome. I'd also be the one to throw a balled-up piece of paper at you if you walked by my desk without saying hello.

Recently (meaning a lifetime ago before I had Parker), I went into a meeting and met some new employees. Someone introduced us and while I was shaking their hands I said, "I obviously had sex and will be leaving for three months soon."

It's a precautionary measure. I make people laugh, so if they catch a mistake while I'm gone, they'll forgive me. And yes, I embarrassed myself and the new employees, but it's done and now I'm officially on said maternity leave. Because I had sex.

I know I overwhelm people, but I don't have a dimmer switch. Here's the deal: I get other people to laugh and lighten up because then I will have a permission slip to do the same. It's a win-win situation.

Okay, back to the issue of my screaming, pissed-off infant. It's a matter of monkey see, monkey do. I guess you could say I'm a little in-your-face. So it makes sense that Parker is in my face screaming all the time. Like me, if she's in a room, you'll know she's there.

May 24, 2000

Molly, my best friend since 6th grade had her baby

a couple weeks before I had mine. Her baby sleeps all the time and only cries when she's hungry. Molly is getting naps and sleeping through the night already. Basically the only difference in her life is the bouncy seat in her living room - which never gets used, by the way, because she doesn't need it. Molly can lay her daughter on a blanket and she just lays there. Totally content. I didn't even know that kind of baby existed.

Molly's been watching movies, having people over, and going out to Happy Hours. I'm lucky if I brush my teeth. A whole movie! She watches actual movies. You've got to be kidding me. In fact, yesterday she told me that she's bored on her maternity leave because her baby doesn't do anything. "I feed her and she sleeps forever. I'm sick of watching movies all day."

She's sick of watching movies all day. That's her maternity leave. If her life could have a title right now it would be, "Maternity Movie Madness."

Want to know what my title would be? "Screaming From Hell."

May 25, 2000

I've been picking up my old journals and re-living who I was before I was pregnant, before this mountainous event of having a child occurred. I want to smell the pages and bask in the freeness of it all. Of the days when I was available and unconstrained, to do anything and everything at

Un-Perfect

a moment's notice...but never did.

People always told me, "You better enjoy your life now before kids." But the truth is, Derek and I were already living like parents. At 25, I was an old person in a young person's body. Obnoxious and loud, yes, but I was responsible beyond my years.

When we graduated from college, we lived in apartments in a suburb instead of downtown. Why? Because I thought that was what responsible people did. We didn't randomly jet off to Mexico, we didn't party every weekend and we never played hooky from work to enjoy a day of drinking in the sun.

Never.

Why the hell didn't we have sex on the kitchen counter, jet off to Brazil and party in Seattle with totally awesome live bands? WHY?!?

And now I can't. Ever.

Or at least until I'm 50, which will not be the same as if I did it in my twenties.

Well, that door is shut.

After I graduated from college, I had a job within a week. I searched for a job desperately, like a widowed mother with five kids. I was a receptionist at a tractor supply company and hated it, but it was responsible and steady. Why was

Kelly Nordstrom

I responsible and steady when I didn't have a family to be responsible and steady *for*? Because it felt safe and secure. I like structure. No, I *love* structure. So a child is a perfect fit for me. Feedings, naps, diaper changes…perfect. Everything in my life has been perfect. Even the day Derek proposed:

August 21, 1994

It happened! Derek proposed yesterday at my state softball tournament. I was playing right center, meanwhile D was putting up a 50-foot banner that read, "KELLY WILL YOU MARRY ME?" I was crying so hard I could barely breathe. I tried yelling, "YES!" a couple times, but I was so choked up, he couldn't hear me. It was perfect. Everything felt right. Perfect timing, perfect day (73 and sunny!), and our parents were there. Dad videotaped it. Everything I dreamed it would be.

The team we were playing against yelled, "WELL? WHAT DID YOU SAY?" I just gave a thumbs-up because I was still crying. Everyone started yelling and clapping. What an experience – a beautiful experience. Derek, you're the love of my life!

I didn't play the rest of the tournament. Instead, we escaped in his Honda Civic, on which he wrote, "JUST ENGAGED" in soap all over the windows. People on the street honked their horns at us and I flashed my sparkly diamond at them, pointing to the evidence. We laughed all the way to the bar, where we met my girlfriends for beers and showed off my ring. Still today, when I look at

Un-Perfect

my left hand I think, "Someone in this world chose me. Out of everyone on this planet, Derek chose *me*. He loves me." I remember driving with my left hand hanging out the window for months to casually show the world that I was chosen. I was going to be Derek's WIFE. Married, just as I had always planned.

Even though Derek and I were dating other people, I steamrolled us together, leaving my boyfriend and his girlfriend wondering what happened. To this day, I feel guilty about that. I was so focused on getting together with Derek that I didn't care who I stepped on to get to him. Our exes were shell-shocked and sad, but I didn't even bother looking back to apologize to their sad faces. I got what I wanted. I got Derek.

When I get focused on things, I tend to rocket full speed ahead, not giving a crap about other people. I can be tenacious when I want to be. I know what I want, so I go out and get it. With intentions so focused, how can I not get what I want in life? If I want something, I work my ass off to get it. "Done and doner", as I always say.

Getting married was something I knew I wanted in life. There was no way I wasn't going to get married and have a family. It's just what I had always dreamed of and expected. When I was ten years old, I'd sit in my bright yellow bedroom and wonder what my future husband was doing at that exact moment. *How old is he? Is he riding a BMX bike? Does he have a paper route? Does he hate math like me? Can he feel me thinking about him? Do I already know him or has he seen me at the mall and didn't know I'm his future wife?* I was already planning my life with excruciating detail. *Who would I marry? How many children would I have? What would I do for a living? How much money would I make?*

Most girls that age are dreamers. They imagine a glamorous life as a professional figure skater or princess. I wanted to be an architect. That speaks volumes about who I am.

But while I've always been incredibly serious, I've also worked hard to go against that seriousness. For that reason, I'm usually the extrovert in the center of the spotlight, verbally tap dancing for everyone's entertainment. Because if I sink into my serious core, then I fear I won't have friends and an extrovert needs friends like a meth addict needs meth. So in high school I usually found myself in uncomfortable predicaments, like running from cops at a keg party in a cornfield or smoking cigarettes at a park while sitting on the monkey bars. I'd steal whiskey from my parent's liquor cabinet and pour it into my lunch thermos and drink it from a straw at football games. I tried hard looking like a rebel.

In college, my roommates would make fun of me because of the daily lists I'd write. Frankly, they had reason to ridicule: "Wake. Go to bank. Work out. Bar." They'd laugh and say, "Really? You need to remind yourself to wake-the-fuck up?" Of course I didn't, but just by waking up, I got to cross something off my list. I was already productive by opening my eyes. That's the beginning of a successful day when you complete a task by rolling out of bed.

To be honest, drinking wasn't really something I loved to do, but it was what everyone else wanted to do. So I fell down stairs and barfed right along with them - just to be part of a group. They were fun and irresponsible and I hoped their carelessness would rub off on me. As hard as I tried, I could never have a one-night stand or skip class. It went against everything I know to be true and good.

For my freshman year, I chose a dorm that kicked you out if you didn't maintain a 3.0 average (it has since been lowered to 2.25, which I think is bullshit). Anyway, there's a reason for that. I could always use it as an excuse to bow out of a night of partying because, "You guys, if I don't ace this test on Wednesday, I could be kicked out of my dorm."

I take everything seriously and when I try to let loose, it just feels wrong. Like my skin is too big for my body, weighing on me. Too much, too big, too heavy. I have a need to pare down, be lean, and totally prepared for anything that

Un-Perfect

comes my way.

And it works for me. I haven't been caught off-guard for anything in my life. Except of course Parker's screaming which has not been miraculously cured by replacing her manhole of a pacifier. I thought for sure that would fix it, but no such luck. She's pissed all the time. We have our first Well Visit tomorrow, thank God. If anyone can fix this, it's the pediatrician. He'll know what to do and everything will go back to perfect again.

May 26, 2000

First Well Visit today.

Derek and I made a list of all our questions:

> *Is pooping three times a day enough?*
>
> *Why isn't she happy?*
>
> *She never naps. Ever. Normal?*
>
> *Freckle on her finger - skin cancer?*

We're going to try a new formula to help with her screaming. We'll just have to find one that works well with her system to make her less gassy, therefore less screamy.

This last question came up this morning. As we were getting ready, Derek noticed a spot on her pointer finger. Neither of us had seen it before, so of course we wondered if babies are even born with freckles and moles. Birthmarks yes, but freckles? Neither of us had seen a freckled baby before, so we were convinced it was skin cancer.

Kelly Nordstrom

The check-up went fine and then the moment of truth. Did she have cancer? I was already picturing myself in a cancer unit with the smallest patient in the world. I'd be trying to hold back tears as they poked and prodded my sweet, screaming 1-week-old baby, holding her tiny defective finger.

The doctor examined her while we held our breath, looking at each other and back to the doctor. This could be news that changed our lives forever. We were ready. He rubbed her finger, looked up and said, "Oh, it's just chocolate."

Shit.

I forgot I ate Junior Mints during the 4:00 a.m. feeding. I fed her with my eyes closed while shoving fistfuls into my mouth. One must have fallen on her or they got all melty. Those damn Junior Mints.

I should switch to M&Ms. They don't melt in your hands like all the other candy out there. M&Ms are definitely the way to go. Or maybe a banana. But I hate fruit. I really hate going to breakfast meetings because there's a tray full of fruit…and then one doughnut that no one touches.

I know I should be a grown up and eat fruit, but I'd rather have the chocolate doughnut. Fruit is so acidic and makes my mouth pucker. Yuck. And it never fails that when I tell someone I don't like fruit, they start listing off all the fruits to make sure they understand my aversion to it clearly.

"What about strawberries, you don't like strawberries?"

"No."

"Oranges? C'mon, how can you refuse an orange?"

"I can't stand oranges or anything orange flavored."

"You're kidding."

"No. I'm not kidding."

"Okay, watermelon. Do you like that?"

Un-Perfect

"No, not really. The seeds are still in there - it's under-done."

"Ever tried a mango?"

"No, I don't want to try a mango."

People work so hard to try and convert me. They refuse to believe that someone is fruit-averse. And then they try to find the root of the cause. Maybe I ate a bunch of fruit and got the flu so I associate bad things with it. Maybe I'm allergic to it. And the answer is no and no. I simply do not like fruit. I'd rather have Junior Mints, which is now going to be replaced with M&Ms, for breakfast, while I'm on maternity leave.

By the way - is it still considered breakfast if you never actually went to sleep the night before? To me, it could just be considered a late-night treat...

I'm up all night checking her chest to make sure she's conscious. Sometimes, if I don't see or hear her breathing, I'll start tapping her shoulders or tickling her face to get some kind of reaction so I know she's still alive. This backfires quite a bit because she wakes up and wants to eat. That part sucks, but at least I know she's still living.

After all the tickling and manipulating, when she starts screaming, I run back into bed and pretend to sleep. I just wanted to make sure she was living, I didn't sign up for an hour-long feeding. I'll elbow Derek in the gut and say, "I just got her, it's your turn."

My poor husband. He has no idea I sneak out of the room to check on her, which usually results in her waking up for a feeding. He's so tired, he doesn't know which end is up, so he believes me.

I know, I'm awful. He'll stagger out of the room saying, "Really? I could swear I just fed her..."

Really, honey. You did just feed her.

Which brings us back to the Well Visit, because indeed she is magically still alive and cancer-free. It was chocolate on her finger, not a tumor. To this statement, we said what any parent in our situation would say:

"We're obviously too stupid to have a child, but since she's here, we'll take her home to figure this out. Thanks."

We drove home in silence, wondering which one of us was going to step up to the plate on this whole parenting thing. Being the mom, you'd think I would be the one to take charge, but I haven't. I didn't even own up to the Junior Mints debacle. Instead, I looked around the doctor's office, pretending to be totally mystified by how chocolate made its way onto our newborn.

"I have no idea how that would happen. Maybe my niece had chocolaty fingers from her birthday party a few days ago?"

I didn't fool anyone.

5/28/00 *Sunday Muffins at Mom's*

Sunday Muffins at Mom's house today. We have this tradition that started when my sisters and I went to Sunday school. Dad would drop us off at church, barely slowing the car down before bolting home. An hour later, he was there to pick us up. It was never a question if my parents were going to church or not. They didn't go and frankly, I wanted it that way.**

It was always such a relief to get home. Church smelled like old people. It made me uncomfortable. I didn't like the smell of church. So every Sunday when I got home, I would race through the front door to see Mom flipping pancakes. She'd have my plate and juice on the table ready for me. "Hi honey!" she'd say as she set out the bacon. "How was Sunday School?" I'd say, "Smelled like old people. Any pancakes ready to go?"

Some Sundays were extra special, when Grandma, Dad's mom, made her infamous sticky buns. One time my sister Kim came home after a party and slathered a sticky bun with "frosting." Turns out it was bacon grease. We still give her crap about it.

Other Sundays Grandma would make chocolate chip cookies for Dad and he'd hide them in the freezer. I didn't touch them because I knew it wasn't just about the cookies. I think he felt special each time he opened the freezer to see them in there. I ate everything else in the house but those cookies.

Anyway, we made it to muffins at Mom's with Parker today for the first time. It was kind of special walking through that front door with my daughter. I've been walking through it since I was seven. I've opened it with a black eye, a broken wrist, roller skates, a broken heart, a soaring heart, a prom dress, boyfriends, a wedding dress, my first paycheck, and now my child. Each time I walked through that door, I was getting a little closer to who I am today. And today I walked through it with my wailing daughter.

All my nieces and nephews were scared to death of her since she screamed the entire time.

Jake, my fifteen year old nephew asked, "So, uh, still think this was a good idea?" My dad looked at her and said, "Is your mean mommy pinching you again? You want me to pinch her back for you?" And actually, yes, I did need a good pinch to make sure I wasn't dreaming. I certainly felt like I was sleeping, or had I just not slept in two or three days? Could that be possible? Had I actually not slept since *Friday*? Shit. I need to stop checking on Parker through the night and get some rest. Every morning I'm stunned that she made it through another night. I'll hear little squeaks and think, "She lived another whole day! I can't believe it!"

Kari, my oldest sister said, "Oh my God. And I thought Holly was a bitch!" (Referring to her daughter who also had colic). They still have a hole in the wall from when Kari

Un-Perfect

lost her cool and rammed her fist through the sheetrock. Their first baby, Jake, was a godsend. Easy, peasy, lemon squeezy. I honestly don't ever remember him crying unless he was physically hurt.

Kim, the middle sister, said "Just hang in there. I know it's hard, but I promise, it will get better." Hanna, her daughter, was one year old now and was nudging her head into Parker's belly like she was pillow. Kim has been blessed with three good, happy babies in total. I can't imagine what that would be like and I'm thankful she didn't rub it in that her kids are better behaved than mine.

Dennis, Kari's husband pointed at Parker's car seat and said, "Yeah, good luck with that. Thank God I don't have to do it again."

Pete, Kim's husband, stared at Parker with eyes as wide as a plate. Speechless. He just shook his head.

My mother looked at Parker and said, "Oh for goodness sake! What is there to be so mad about?"

Everyone, including my nephews, took turns trying to calm her down. Corey is fourteen and God bless him, he was dipping her head almost upside down and back. That was his version of rocking her in his arms. I have to admit, it kind of worked. We passed her around like a relay baton. "Here, YOU try!" I shoved a couple blueberry muffins in my mouth and called it a day. We strapped her back into the car seat and took her home. Why should everyone have to suffer?

** I was breaking one of the Ten Rules all the time - I was drenched in fear and guilt every day – I'd go to bed apologizing for everything: "I'm sorry I cheated at Monopoly, I'm sorry I lied to Mom about having 1 cupcake, I'm sorry I thought about kissing David Hansen, I'm sorry I said 'shit' today – oh great, I just said it again, does that count? Now I have to be double good tomorrow - that's impossible, I'm sorry for living because I'm not doing it right."

It's the religious dogma that got me into trouble. I simply can't NOT question everything. Even when I was twelve. I remember raising my hand to ask, "But how do you know babies don't go to Heaven if they're not baptized?" "What if a gay person is nicer than a married person – does he still go to H-E-double-toothpicks?" I never got anywhere with my pastor and I know I was a pain in the ass, but I'm a seeker. I'm wired to scrutinize, negotiate, and get 360 degrees of an answer..

Plus, I cheated on my confirmation test. It feels so good to finally set this secret free. I've` been holding it in since 1986. My entire class had the answers written on our hands during our verbal test in front of the congregation on the day we were confirmed. But to be fair, our teacher gave us the answers, so he was an accomplice to the crime.

May 29, 2000

She spits up her entire bottle every time I feed her. She simply opens her mouth and barfs it back out. She doesn't even care. One second she's laying down looking

Un-Perfect

around and the next, a tidal wave of formula is pouring out of her face.

Maybe it's the vibrating bouncy seat she lives in? But I can't give that up. It's the only thing that gives me tiny pockets of peace.

I can see how this going to look five years from now, making special peanut butter and jelly sandwiches shaped into perfect little hearts or she won't touch it. I can see her crossing her arms across her chest saying, "MOM, you KNOW I won't touch crust. Fix it!"

She's been here for ten days and we are already trying our third formula. The current formula is soy. Which, by the way, smells like barf before it's even barfed up.

Everything I got at the baby shower is ruined. All of her cute clothes are stained, so I'm dressing her in the ugly ones. Her wardrobe doesn't even match most of the time because it's like "musical clothes." Whatever gets ruined, needs changing. It could be her socks, hat, shirt, or pants. Somewhere along the day, she ends up kind of matched because I go through so many rounds of apparel.

Lately, I'm dressing her in a swimsuit and socks. The less layers, the better because there is nothing worse than pulling a puked-on onesie over her head. That requires a bath. So a bikini is a great way to avoid that mess.

The spitting-up is probably due to the formula feeding, so now the guilt of not breastfeeding is piling up. And now it's too late. My boobs are hanging

Kelly Nordstrom

from my chest like used condoms. The breastaurant is officially closed. And now I'm questioning the reasons I had for declining the breastfeeding route.

I wanted to have Derek bond with her too by feeding her.
I wanted to take turns through the night so I could get a block of sleep.
I needed my allergy medications so I don't blow my nose right off my face.
I had serious concerns about my AAA cups actually providing enough food to sustain a human being.

But now these reasons don't seem to be enough for other mothers. I seriously might slap the next mother that approaches me and says, "Oh, you're NOT breastfeeding? Why?" Where is the love, ladies? I'm a mother too even if I'm not the titty fairy.

Breastfeeding seems to be the only thing new mothers want to talk about. I need to know about big shit, like curing colic, and they're ranting about their cracked nipples. I get it, it's difficult. It's painful. But so is listening to constant screaming all day long. There seems to be a line drawn in the sand as soon as I start talking about formula. Shoulders get a little cooler and they seem to even stand a little further from me as if formula breeds a contagious disease.

I support their choice to breastfeed, why can't my choice be supported too? Some of these women are acting as if I'm killing my baby. One mother said, "I just question why you wouldn't want the best for your baby."

A verbal smack down ensued right there at my friend's baby shower. I said, "I'm happy with my choice and I'm not judging yours. We'll have to agree to disagree." I wanted to punch her in the face.

It felt good to (appear to) take the non-judgmental high road, but as I

Un-Perfect

walked away I muttered, "Bitch" under my breath.

What can I say, I've always been a passive-aggressive kind of gal.

May 30, 2000

I feel sucker punched. All the new moms out there are smiling and happy with their babies in their Bjorns. What are they so happy about? They're always holding hands with their husbands. I barely recognize Derek through this fatigued haze.

Personally, I feel like it was Bait-and-Switch. I fell for it. I saw them and wanted to be one of them. And now this is what all the fuss was about? This is what looked so awesome? I didn't see this coming at all.

The constant demands and needs of a newborn are overwhelming. I feel like I was punched to the ground and I can't brush off my knees and get up. I'm exhausted.

It's constant. I can't put her in the Bjorn and leave her be - I have to bounce her while she's strapped in. I can't just take her for a walk, I have to jigger the stroller so much it's probably shaking her brain against her skull and causing brain damage.

She doesn't sit in her car seat in a restaurant, I have to stand and swing it back and forth until she almost falls out of it. I hate that none of the Mom Tricks work for me. Everyone suggests I take her for a drive. That's bullshit.

She screams the entire time unless I drive over a particularly bumpy road. The other day I was at a red light and I looked at the car next to me. The driver was about twenty, jamming to his music. I had earplugs in trying to dilute the hysteria and stay calm. I desperately wanted to switch places with him.

It's a Mom Cult. Either those women only keep it together while they're in public and bawl their eyes out when they get home, or they're totally faking. I know this because I'm a new mom and this fucking sucks. It is so hard.

Having a baby is like walking over a landmine. Boom! My entire being has been blown away and now I'm left picking up all the "Kelly pieces" lying all over the floor. I don't know who I am, who I'm supposed to be, or who I want to be. When will I be me again?

Or a more terrifying thought, *will* I ever be me again?

I'm trying to make myself whole again because I'm all over the place. Blown apart and overwhelmed by this entire situation called motherhood. I think there's something about the firstborn that shatters a mother, dissecting her life with a line of pre-motherhood and post-motherhood. And maybe there is no going back.

Parker is the one in the driver's seat, totally understanding everything about this mother/daughter situation. She's an infant and gets it. I'm a 30-year-old woman left feeling broken and confused.

And what's worse, I'm too tired to give a shit.

June 2, 2000

I have to run errands today, but I can't figure out which order makes the most sense. Should I tackle Target first since it's a farther drive away and work my way back

Un-Perfect

home or should I go to Cub first to get groceries and beat the after-work rush hour? Wait, where is the post office again? I have to mail these Thank You cards before everyone thinks I'm rude.

Every gift I receive I think, "Oh great, another Thank You card I'm going to have to write and mail." I don't mean to be ungrateful, but the pressure to keep up with etiquette is insufferable. Screw the cute onesies, I wish someone would give me a big packet of stamps so I don't have to scramble around trying to find one when I have to mail yet another motherfucking Thank You card.

Maybe I should shower before running errands, but I want to get to Cub before it gets too busy. I can't figure out which place I'd rather be at when the screaming hits the hardest. Post office? But it's such a small place; everyone would be so annoyed. In the car? But I hate driving with ear plugs because I think it's unsafe.

Argh, I can't figure out how my day should go, so I just sit here and write in this journal. Whatever decision I make will be the wrong one anyway.

I'm not doing anything right. Dinners are insane. I can't possibly figure out if Derek should pick up McDonalds or if I should try and cook while soothing a screaming baby. I can't cook with her in the Baby Bjorn because she could start on fire. My God, that would be awful. Anyway, Derek called and asked what I wanted for dinner, but I have no idea, so he rambled through a list: "Chinese? No. Mexican? Uh, I don't think so. Burgers? No, definitely not burgers. Unless YOU want burgers, then I guess it's fine. It really doesn't matter to me. You pick." He sighed and I knew he was frustrated. I should've just picked one and pretended to be confident about it.

Whatever decision I make, I'll wish I picked something else anyway.

June 2, 2000 Bedtime

It's seems like everyone is trying to pull me away from Parker. Why don't they understand that I just want to stay in my home, sans visitors, and just BE? I just want to be alone. With my daughter. I don't want anyone taking her from me so I can rest. Why doesn't anyone understand that?

When I leave the house, my heart races and I can't breathe. Running into friends at the grocery store is awful. They start talking and cooing at Parker, but I can't comprehend what they're saying because I need to rush through the lines before Parker starts screaming. They don't understand that she is a ticking time bomb.

It feels like everyone is trying to distract me from being a mom. They want me to get rest, they want to visit, and they want to take her from me so I

Un-Perfect

can run errands ALONE. I don't want to be away from her. Why does everyone think I want to be away from my daughter?

When friends and family come to visit, I'm stuck, like someone hit the Pause button on my life. I feel like I can't share special moments with Parker while other people are staring at me. They just stare and I feel judged. So I don't hug or kiss her when I'm around other people.

And I REALLY hate it when they take her from me so they can hold her. Everyone on this planet wants to hold my baby. I barely answer the door and they have their arms outstretched to grab her from me. My chest feels cold and empty when they pull her off my body. I'm her mom - I want to hold her too. The entire time someone else is holding her, I'm fidgeting, hoping she cries so I can take her back.

And all these people, they just make it worse. They hold her too loosely and they don't bounce her right. They're doing it wrong and God knows if they have a cold or the flu and they're just pretending to be healthy. I ask them to put hand sanitizer on their hands and they look at me like, "Give me a fucking break." Where's the respect? No one seems to respect me as a mother.

Every second is so precious and each time someone comes over, they rob me of that time with my daughter. I don't answer the phone anymore – I hope everyone just goes away and leaves Parker and I alone.

June 3, 2000

How did I get here, walking around my living room, bouncing a hollering baby in my arms all day? Wasn't it just yesterday that I was slamming down shots of tequila in college and calling everyone an asshole?

I barely survived on my own through college, so I'm not sure why I thought I could be accountable for another person's life. I think I should've eased into this "being-responsible-for-life" thing with maybe a fish, then a puppy, then a human being. You know, give myself a chance to evolve with the maturity process.

But no, I'm an over-achiever, so I went for the gold right away. A real live human being. Completely and totally dependent on me. I can't even remember to take the garbage out on Tuesdays, how am I going to keep her alive? Not to mention trying to keep her happy which, by the way, is requiring herculean effort on my part.

I look at all the women in the grocery store and wonder how they keep it all together. They cook, wash dishes, change diapers, take out the trash, meet friends for lunch, pick up dry cleaning, bathe their children, shower... how do they do it all? What is their secret? And they don't seem stressed at all. They know what they're doing without any instruction.

I keep looking for a bullet-pointed list for me to check things off and this list doesn't exist. I'm a follower, not a leader. I like to walk the tried and true path that everyone else walks. But I don't know what others are doing, so there's no one to follow.

Un-Perfect

It reminds me of the time I ran a 5k race and came in last. I don't run. Ever. I have no idea why I thought I could (or even should) run in a race. I wasn't even running in running shoes. I just grabbed my black Reebok high tops and entered the race out of the blue. I guess it was because I was at the bar drinking and everyone was bragging about running and I thought they were being a little dramatic about the level of difficulty. Big deal. You put one foot in front of the other. We learned this skill when we were 18 months old.

I was hacking and wheezing and swore the entire 3.2 miles. It was the worst fifty minutes of my life. The cones were being pulled up because apparently there's a time limit and I was dragging ass. I couldn't tell where I was going without the cones. So I just walked around with my humiliating numbered bib still pinned to my chest. I was alone with no one to follow.

I need cones, people! Bright orange cones to mark my way and give me a signal when I run off course. I feel like the lone mother running this race.

I seem to be the only mother that is:

A). Not obsessed with breastfeeding.

B). Has a colicky baby.

I'm not connecting with anyone on a lot of levels. I don't know what I'm doing and the books on babies are insane. They all conflict each other. Bathe once a week or bathe every other day. Let the baby sleep with you or you could suffocate the baby by co-sleeping. I can't figure it out and nothing necessarily feels good to me. I want to do it right, but honestly, I'm in survival mode, so tummy time and shit like that is just gravy. I'm just trying not to pass out from exhaustion.

There are no books on colic, other than medical case studies. I am my own case study. Nothing seems to match my experience. I need support. I need someone, anyone, to tell me they've been here to this place and it gets better. I want to sit with them over a cup of coffee and hear their story. I need to know that someone has survived this debilitating scream-a-palooza.

I'm a person who needs to be accepted and approved. When we go to a party and someone doesn't seem to like me, it bothers me for weeks. I'm at their mercy, force-feeding my good nature to them because I can't stand the thought of someone not liking me. It's painful to realize that my own daughter doesn't like me. I'm taking it personally.

I'm lonely and judged. People stare at me like, "Why the hell are you letting your daughter scream like that?" One stranger suggested that I feed her since she's "*obviously starving*." I said, "She's not hungry, she's colicky. I just fed her. I don't know what to do." The woman shrugged and nodded her head back and forth like I'm a lost case.

She's right. I'm lost.

6/4/00 Sunday Muffins at Mom's

When I walked through the front door, everyone turned to see if a tornado just blew in. Nope, it's just me and my bundle of incessant screaming. I heard them mutter, "poor thing" and "holy shit" over the yelling and spitting up.

I took my seat at the counter, swinging the car seat back and forth while trying to butter my blueberry muffin. Finally, I just gave up and let Mom do it for me since my arms were aching so bad. She looked at me and said, "Does she ever quit? I mean,

Un-Perfect

doesn't she get tired?"

Kari, my oldest sister chimed in and said, "Yeah, you'd think she'd just pass out. I mean, *look at her*, she's *purple* from crying so hard."

I don't know how Kari is sitting here today with her pre-teen daughter looking so normal after dealing with a screaming baby like mine. And she did it without help, which sets the expectation bar for me. I can't ask for help because then I'll be less than Kari and I fear I'll lose out on the sibling competition and my parents will like her more than me.

I need to be strong and independent because that is what is expected of me. I don't know how it worked out, but Kari handled her screaming daughter without any help from anyone. I hardly remember hearing about it, so she didn't complain about it either. How the hell did she do that? There's no way I can ask for help now that she made it through without assistance or complaining.

Everyone will come to my rescue and Kari will resent me for it because no one rescued her. I can't break up the equality of attention and care like that. No way. Everything has been fair between the three daughters since the day we were born.

Even now, my mother stuffs our Christmas stockings with the exact same gifts. She even counts them to make sure everything is Even Steven. We say we don't care, but honestly, if Kim got six Christmas gifts and I got three, I'd worry my parents love her more than me.

It goes like this: Whatever the firstborn does, the bumpers of what is expected and accepted are set up. Kari didn't complain and she didn't ask for help. I'm certainly not going to be the first one to wave a white flag and yell, "UNCLE!" when everyone else in my family has handled their own challenges independently.

My sister Kim had a son when she was a sophomore in college and not only did she get her Bachelor's degree, but her she got her Master's degree without any help from anyone. In fact, she moved further away from us, instead of closer, just to prove that she could do it alone.

It's like we welcome the challenge to prove how strong and independent we are. Mom remembers going over to Kim's apartment and found her cupboards bare, so she bought truckloads of food for Kim and her son. But

Un-Perfect

why didn't she ask? My parents are so willing to help, so why don't we reach for their hand in time of need? Because we're so busy competing in the "Battle Of The Sisters"? Trying to prove that we're the strongest, hence the best one?

For me, personally, I feel like I would be the black sheep of the family. Everyone is so smart, beautiful and totally together that no one has had to step up to the plate and say, "Yeah, my life is sucking wind right now. Can you give me a helping hand here?" It would be like stepping forward with a bullhorn and ruining a perfect family.

June 7, 2000

I cannot figure out why I deserve a healthy baby and others don't. It's not fair. Those women would probably be better mothers than me and appreciate motherhood more than me. They wouldn't crumple and get upset like I do.

Those women don't get to have children, but I do??? How did that happen? I feel like I slipped through the cracks when God wasn't looking. I feel like He took a coffee break, came back and said, "Oh you've got to be kidding me - who let Kelly Nordstrom on the mom list? She's going to screw this up, huge."

I ran away for fifteen minutes today. I slammed the front door shut and sat on the front step, headphones blasting at full volume to drown out the incessant screaming.

It was heaven. Fresh air. Music. I almost wish I smoked because I think a cigarette would have really hit the spot... Inhale a little poison and just be a bad girl for once instead of trying to do the right thing all the time.

I know that fifteen minutes was too long, but I also knew that if I went back in the house, I might not be able to restrain my anger. So Parker had to wait while I listened to Rob Thomas sing "Bent."

If I fall along the way, I hope to God someone picks me up and dusts me off. I'm feeling completely Bent. I hope somewhere along this road, I get put back together. I never knew that Rob and I had so much in common. It makes me wonder what he's been through to even communicate these lyrics that ring so true. These feelings of being lost are obviously not limited to mothering a colicky baby since Rob Thomas is in fact not a woman. But what else could possibly be this bad to cause feelings of being Bent and broken? I can't imagine what else could rip a person apart like this.

Anyway, she didn't wait patiently. Everything was soaked with sweat and puke when I went back in to get her. Sheets, bikini, hair. Her voice was even hoarse from screaming so hard. She was pissed that I left her in there, and I don't blame her, but I was at the end of my rope. I can't believe I left her in the house, crying *all alone*, for fifteen minutes. I'm a horrible mom.

Un-Perfect

But I had to get away for just that snippet of time and take care of myself for once. Just be by myself without someone on me. I feel like I'm Velcro and everyone is made of felt material. They just stick on me. If it's not Derek and Parker, then people are popping over to visit and they tend to stick too. I don't like people clinging to me because I don't know how to direct, lead, or guide them.

I hate it when people come to visit because they have a front row seat to witness my failure. They stare at me while I go down in flames, trying to cover it up with a smile and a joke. But it's no joke. I'm so embarrassed that I can't get it right and now everyone that comes to visit knows my secret: I'm a failure as a mother. I hate that people know I'm not perfect.

June 9, 2000

I wake up every morning around 4:00 am with an anxiety attack and I hate it because there's no controlling it.

It controls me. As soon as I'm aware that I'm awake, my heart pounds and I get hot. I kick off the covers, but then I get cold. I don't know why this happens. The day hasn't even begun, why panic?

But I can't stop it. The pounding heart, the hots, and then for some reason, this brings on an allergy attack. Apparently I'm allergic to anxiety? My chest gets tight, my nose plugs up, my throat itches and my face starts swelling, so this requires me to get up and take a Benadryl.

I attempt going back to sleep, but I start worrying about money, wondering why I'm such a bad mom, or if my panties were bunched up over my jeans at Target yesterday.

I have a desperate need to find a reason to be embarrassed or things to worry about. Even when there's nothing. I try to settle myself down and go back to sleep, thinking "You're tucked into a warm bed and nothing is happening now. Go to sleep."

But it doesn't work. I blow my nose, sweat, and listen to my pounding heart until the Benadryl kicks in and knocks me out.

I would love to wake up peacefully, taking in a full breath and not fast-forward through the next twenty-four hours. A lot of the days feel like déjà vu. I've already lived them in my head, complete with frantic lullabies, headaches, and dithering over past due bills. Why can't we just be wealthy? Everything would be fine if we had money. I could hire a nurse to live with us. I heard celebrities have live-in nurses that take the nightshifts. Why couldn't I be a celebrity?

I gnaw at the insides of my cheeks while I pre-play the day in my head. I pinch the flesh with my teeth until I break through the skin, until my teeth can touch without anything in the way. Bone on bone. Then I run my tongue over the inflicted area to feel the angry bumps I left there. I try to concentrate on making a perfect line of bruises on the insides of my cheeks.

I don't know why I do this. I've always done it. As a teenager, I'd take my fingernail and push down the gums until the pain was intense. I'd do it while studying for tests.

Un-Perfect

Now I just suck in my cheeks and start biting. If I get lost driving, I do the cheek-biting. If I'm in a fight with Derek, I bite my cheeks. If I'm panicking about Parker's screaming, I score a row of tortured wounds. Logically, it doesn't help my situation, but it gives me something to focus on while I think about finding my way.

6/18/00 Sunday Muffins At Mom's

When you walk through the door of Mom and Dad's house, you're on immediate display for everyone sitting at the kitchen counter to see you. So I have to gear up, wipe away my tears of despair and slap a smile on my face as soon as I open the door. And I open the door and I smell that smell. My parents' house. I feel so safe and secure here. I want to crawl up the stairs to my old bedroom and sleep for a month.

The room has changed quite a bit, but I can still picture the corkboard wall full of pictures of my friends and me. The "Purple Rain" poster with Prince sitting on his purple motorcycle was just across the room from my bed. I remember my mom walking in, arms full of folded laundry, and asking, "Who is that little black man on the motorcycle?"

I want someone to fold my laundry again. I want someone to take care of me.

But it's time to take care of my daughter. So I swing her car seat and let Mom butter my blueberry muffin for me. Then all the women want to take a turn to see if they can calm Parker down, but she only gets worse and they hand her back to me saying, "Yeah, she doesn't like this."

Yeah, I know.

She doesn't like anything and now you're handing her back to me. Since I'm the mom, I'm supposed to know what to do. And I don't. I don't know what to do.

They all watch me as I try to calm this little grenade down while standing in the spotlight. Then comments start:

"Poor baby, what can be so bad when you're only a month old?"

"Man, is she pissed off!"

God, what *is* so bad when you're only a month old?

Having a mom like me. There. That's the answer.

June 20, 2000

This is my life now. I bounce Parker around the house for twelve hours every day. I don't go anywhere because

Un-Perfect

people look at me like I'm doing a bad job. They are right. I am doing a bad job.

I should be excited to see Parker's beautiful blue eyes, but all I do is cringe. And wait. It's like pulling in my last breath, waiting for a soldier to pull the trigger while I'm tied to a pole. An execution. I can't escape and I know the assault is coming. And there's nothing I can do to prevent it.

I'm frightened of my own kid. Moms aren't supposed to be scared, are they?

She opens her eyes and the bullets hit my heart. It's like she says, "Good morning. You're a horrible mom." She's pissed all the time.

What can be so bad? I wipe her *ass*, for God's sake. I carry her everywhere and bounce her in my arms all day because if I stop, she screams.

Every day I beg for amnesty. I sing songs, pat her back, change her poopy diapers, burp her, tell her I love her, rub her belly, tip her forward like a football hold, do the bicycle thing with her legs until she farts, and kiss her toes that look like little grapes. What else can I possibly do to please her?

I feel like all day I fill up her bucket, but her bucket is filled with holes. The water leaks out, I keep filling. This continues all day until the magical hour of 10:30 p.m. And for some reason, my work is done and she sleeps. I do not understand this, but I'm grateful she grants me a reprieve from hell.

Derek

7/1/00

I'm tired as hell, but I've got the goods. My wife is hot and my daughter is amazing.

Every little thing in Kel's life is planned and controlled. It's what attracted me to her in college. On her twenty-first birthday, she just walked up to me at the pizza joint where we both worked and declared, "It's my twenty-first birthday today. So are you going to take me out for dinner, dancing, and hot passionate sex?"

This was our first line of communication. I almost dropped everything I was holding. Who was this girl and why was she in my face asking me to celebrate her birthday? Not that I minded, of course. I'd been staring at her for weeks, but never had the courage to even say "hey".

I'm quiet and shy; she's loud and obnoxious. She beats herself up; I don't. She questions every little thing; I let stuff slide. She likes crowds; I hate them.

Social shit makes me crazy. If it wasn't for Kelly, I'd be a hermit. If you paid me a million dollars, I could never walk up to a stranger and introduce myself and start talking about life. No way. But Kelly? Twenty minutes into a party she's made three

Un-Perfect

new friends.

Not that we get out much anymore, which is fine with me. Parker gives me an excuse to hole up and stay home.

But the crying... Holy shit.

Would I have requested to have a baby that cries non-stop? No. Am I going to stress about it? No. It is what it is. Yeah, yeah, I thought she had cancer on her finger and it ended up being chocolate... *that* was embarrassing. I'm still not sure why Kelly didn't just own up to it so we could have a good laugh about it.

We used to laugh all the time.

I miss her singing bad karaoke in the car - it was funny as hell, hearing her belting it out at the top of her lungs, but still not quite reaching the high notes.

I'm not sure I'm helping as much as I should. I know Kel's tired because she whines about it constantly. That pisses me off. We're both tired and I understand that she's home with Parker all day and I'm not. But when I offer to help with anything she says it's fine. Whatever.

It's not rocket science. If a person is tired and someone offers you sleep, you take it. Yesterday, I offered to take Parker for a drive so Kelly can sleep, but she doesn't want to be away from Parker. So I offered to play with Parker on the deck so Kel could take a nap, but she doesn't want that either. I know she's strong and independent. In a way, I'm glad to see that part hasn't been lost. It's who she is (still frustrating though).

Kelly's on a rampage trying to figure out what will make Parker stop crying...the swing, formula, fresh air, burping. Every day she comes up with a new strategy to make the screaming stop. Yesterday she kept a journal of every pee, poop, spit-up and burp and started Parker on Mylicon drops for gas. It looks exhausting.

Note: She's so crazy about finding a cure for colic that I think it's actually wrecking progress, but I don't saying because she'll get pissed.

July 2, 2000

I can't help thinking I have it so good that something bad is going to happen. I think I have cancer, but none of the doctors are catching it. I've been to my OB/GYN and my regular doctor, but both of them say I'm healthy. I think they are missing something. I wanted them to take a blood test, but they said it's not necessary.

It's horrible to think that I could die and leave

Un-Perfect

Parker and Derek alone. I wouldn't be able to hug, kiss and hold and smell them anymore. I wouldn't see her grow up, graduate and get married.

I wonder what it would be like to know I'm dying while holding her - would this be the last time? I have to shed this thinking, but I can't shut it off. I need to enjoy life! And I do, but maybe these thoughts of dying are just to make sure I don't take it all for granted. I've been complaining about the colic, so these thoughts are to make sure that I understand that I really am blessed. Yes, she screams, but she is my healthy, beautiful daughter that is experiencing a momentary lapse in happiness.

My fear is that when I let my guard down, bad things will happen. I've got to be on guard at all times. I want to be Superwoman with her powerful wrist cuffs or whatever she used to ward off villains. I need those cuffs! Not only did they look cool, but they were incredibly practical. They protected her from everything.

What's protecting me from anything out there? I don't have special powers. I could get cancer, pummeled by a bus, contract an unknown killer virus, I could have a brain tumor and not know it.

I'm like a little juicy lamb walking around in Africa while the lions lick their chops. I've got to make sure I'm protected and healthy. I wish there was something like a full body MRI scan. It should be a law that every person should get an annual scan to make sure they are okay.

July 4, 2000

Independence Day. The definition of independence:

"Freedom from control or influence of another or others."
Since my life is controlled and influenced by a newborn, I'm
not independent. I used to be independent, but I'm not
anymore.

Is there anything lonelier in this world than waking
up in the middle of the night for a feeding? I stare out the
windows as I rock and feed her. Black.

I feel like the night folds in on me like that lead
blanket at the dentist's office when you get an x-ray. So
heavy on my chest.

I look at the neighbors' houses thinking, "Is anyone
out there? They're all tucked warmly and safely in their beds
and I'm all alone feeling completely overwhelmed, exhausted
and lonely.

I asked Derek if he feels lonely when he takes the
middle-of-the-night feeding and he said, "Why would I feel
alone? I'm with my daughter."

Yeah, why do I feel so lonely when another person is
right there with me? It doesn't make sense.

I stare out the kitchen window, biting my cheeks, as I rinse out the
bottle. It's all black. No one is awake. I'm not in sync with the rest of the world.
They have cadence and routine and I don't. I always hurry the night feedings
because the loneliness is too much to bear.

Un-Perfect

It's hard to breathe and I realize I'm having an anxiety attack. My sinuses start acting up and I start feeling sick to my stomach. My anxiety attacks become allergy attacks. I need my inhaler, I can't breathe through my nose, I'm wheezy and my face aches. I'm getting sick. I just know it. Again. A couple weeks ago I had pinkeye and now I'll probably get bronchitis. Bronchitis can kill a person if they have asthma. I have asthma. I could die from bronchitis. So many people get bronchitis and don't think anything of it, but if I got it, I could die.

If I'm honest, I like having the excuse of being sick so I can explain why I'm such a bad mom. Plus, if I'm sick, someone will take care of me for once. But if I'm not sick, then I don't have an excuse to accept help and I need to have everything in perfect order. So if I get bronchitis, someone will help me.

No one else seems to need help but me.

Other moms don't seem to mind this suffocating nighttime feeding. It's simply an inconvenience to them. Like flying in planes. "Ugh, I'm going to be so uncomfortable for the next three hours" they say.

I'd give anything to be concerned about my comfort when flying. I'm thinking about life and death, mainly death, thinking the plane is going to fall out of the sky in a fiery explosion. I'm filled with panic when flying. I stare at the flight attendants with such intensity they probably think I will be stalking them after we land. Frankly, I think they put on a brave face when they're actually terrified. Some of those air pockets are frightening and they're still serving juice and water, apologizing for throwing a cup of water in my face because we just dropped five hundred feet *in the fucking sky*. I don't care about water in my face, I do care that 500 tons of metal, meaning this plane, my *life*, just sank in the sky. How does a plane have the power to pull itself back up?

Anyway, the only thing that seems to calm me down after these nighttime feedings/anxiety/allergy attacks is crawling back into bed with Derek and resting my face against his warm back. Then I breathe deep and exhale. I'm not alone.

One more night is done and no matter how many more I have in front of me, I'll never have to do this specific night feeding again. I hope tomorrow night's feeding is at least closer to the sun rising. If the sun is coming up, then people are alive again and I'm not alone in this world. It's that black sky with bright pinholes that creep me out. It's too big for just one small person like me to be looking at it. A vast hole threatening to swallow me.

July 6, 2000

I keep having the same dream over and over again.

It's terrifying. A man breaks into our house and he's walking up the stairs to kill all of us.

Last night I woke up screaming and standing by the wall. Derek was even scared, yelling my name over and over again to wake me up. I was shaking, crying, and sweating as if this happened in real life.

It felt so real, it took a while for me to come back to reality. I hate sleepwalking. It's like sitting on a fence between here in this world and over there in the dream world.

I've always been a sleepwalker, so I know the drill. It's weird waking up in the middle of it because the air feels electric. I can feel every molecule in the air around me.

Anyway, my heart was banging against my ribs,

Un-Perfect

fighting for its life. Worse than my 50-minute 5k race. And to think my mind created such a ruckus for my body.

Who shakes and sweats from a dream? I know it's not real, but I can't stop my body from reacting to it. I'd hate to see what I'd do with a virtual video game. I'd probably need the chest paddles to shock me back to life.

I'm such a psychosomatic sister.

Is everyone? Or is it just me?

Maybe it's only applicable to me, but I can actually make myself sick. It's quite a talent, actually. If I feel pressured to do something I don't want to do, I will achieve a sinus infection, bronchitis, or if it's really important, the flu.

And it's real. There is vomit involved, but I'm convinced that my inability to stand up for myself is what causes it.

My words aren't allowed to come out and play, so they throw a tantrum and make my body sick. Sentences that never make it to the playground are:

"Thanks for the offer, but I'm going to pass."

"That doesn't work for me".

"I'm disappointed you bailed on brunch at the last minute and left me sitting at the restaurant. Alone."

"No. My workload is too heavy to allow more on my plate."

"I need help."

"I'd appreciate you speaking directly with me about any issues you may have, instead of talking behind my back."

I've never been able to stand up for myself. It makes me sick. Literally.

Kelly Nordstrom

I get so worked up. My heart pounds, my hands shake, my breathing is shallow, and I become paralyzed with fear as if my survival is dependent upon telling someone that I can't make it to their eighteenth Pampered Chef party.

Thank God I don't live in a time where hunting animals is a lifestyle. I wouldn't last a minute. "Oh great, here comes a lion and I have *the* worst headache in the world…"

So it makes sense that my dreams affect me the way they do. My mind has a strong somatic effect on me, making me believe that even while I sleep, I'm still in survival mode. It seems impossible to rest my mind and body since I'm fighting off intruders during sleep.

Wait a minute, I just had a thought.

Can I go into cardiac arrest from a bad dream? Sure as hell felt like I could. What would be on my death certificate, "Bad dream"? Seriously. They say if you pee in your dream, you'll wet your bed. So if you dream that you're killed, do you die? Or is that an urban legend? Seems like something I need to know ASAP.

I didn't go back to sleep. There was no way I could go back to sleep when a nightmare like that was waiting for me. I snuggled up next to Derek, hoping his peaceful breathing would be contagious and I'd slip into beautiful oblivion.

It didn't work.

I started cutting rows into the sides of my cheeks, trying to plan when middle-of-the-night feedings would be done. I'm guessing maybe another month, divide that by two since Derek takes half the nights. Two more weeks – I can do this. As I settled on my strategy, my cheeks started to burn and I realized it might be hard to talk tomorrow because I cut them so deep.

Un-Perfect

7/9/00   *Sunday Muffins At Mom's*

We open the front door to display ourselves to everyone sitting at the kitchen counter. This is not just a feeling I have here, it's the feeling of having everyone in the world looking at me and I don't know what I'm doing. This happens everywhere: When I walk into a mommy group, into the pediatrician's office, or even just walking down the street.

I feel people staring at me.

What's upsetting is that I've allowed this feeling to creep into the safest atmosphere I've known, which is my parents' home. My family. We walk in the door and they simply look to see who has arrived. But lately I'm taking it personally or like I'm being attacked, because my heart starts pounding and I just want to make those ten steps to the counter so I can melt in with everyone else and get out of the spotlight.

Their heads turn toward us and shake back and forth in amazement. "She's STILL screaming?" In fact, Kari said that out loud. Pete, Kim's husband looked at us with total shock wondering how we're keeping it together. I still can't ask for help because I refuse to be the weak link in the family.

Everyone has their life together and I'm

not going to be the exception. I'm not going to be the one my parent's friends ask about. "Oh, how is your youngest, the screwed up one?" I refuse to be the conversation piece when my parents or sisters run into people at the grocery store. I refuse to disappoint them.

So Derek and I tag team while we stuff ourselves with breakfast. Dad steps in once in a while to be the breakfast co-pilot with Mom. He makes custom omelets and today was one of those days. It's a beautiful thing since we've been living on toast and cereal. And M&Ms.

What makes his omelets even better is that he whistles while he works. This has always been the case in our family. My sisters and I would make a bet that if I waltzed into the kitchen singing "Oh Suzanna, oh don't you cry for me, 'cuz I come from Alabama with a banjo on my knee" my dad would pick up the tune and start whistling or singing it. Worked every time.

Making breakfast with Dad is like being a co-star in a Broadway musical with him. You just sew together a song, trading off harmony and lyrics without realizing you've just sung a duet.

Un-Perfect

So we eat omelets and blueberry muffins and try to have good conversation while swinging the car seat at an obnoxious speed. Mom's face conveys panic that my infant will fall out, but I know the G-force is too strong for that.

For some reason, Parker seems to enjoy feeling like she's in a tornado. I can't comprehend why swinging her car seat at breakneck speed silences her colic, but it does and I don't question magic.

July 12, 2000

She obviously doesn't understand that I like to have things planned out. I like structure. I like to know the plan, but there is no plan. This drives me crazy. We're "plan-less". I hate it. She just does whatever she wants and I'm a busy satellite orbiting around her, hoping to make her happy.

This is my life now: Catering to an infant.

Yesterday I could only calm her down for 15 minutes all day.

I was bawling right with her. I feel completely beaten down and exhausted. My outlook is bleak, which is very unusual for me. I'm always able to resolve things and strategize and manipulate to make life work for me.

But an infant doesn't understand reasoning and negotiating. An infant just *feels* life, rather than plans it. There is no rhyme, reason, or pattern when it comes to an infant's brain. They need what they need and want what they want. It doesn't matter what the timeline is or if it interrupts anyone else's lives.

Those little babies are so narcissistic. It's all about them.

I didn't think it could get worse and it did. How much worse can it get? I wish she could pull an Excel sheet out of her diaper to show me how she plans on moving forward with this whole screaming business. Each day I think I'm at the end of my rope, and then she adds a few more inches to it. When will we cross the finish line?

This can't go on for much longer. I mean, there is no way she is going scream like this in kindergarten. She wouldn't be allowed to attend school and I'd have to home school her and I suck at geography. I played Pictionary in high school once and put Texas on the East Coast. I'm not qualified to home school anyone.

But it has to pass. I just don't see people screaming and throwing fits in stores or in meetings. Although I have to say, a few colleagues of mine have come close. Their egos are too big for their tiny little life to contain, so it bursts out in a tantrum. In a meeting.

Maybe these people are the adult versions of colicky babies? They never learned how to stop screaming to get what they want.

I don't want Parker to be that bitch in a meeting that everyone hates. I need to teach her some coping mechanisms that don't involve screaming at the top of her lungs. But first I have to begin with myself. I need to figure this out and learn how to handle it with grace instead of wanting to sit on the front step and smoke. Damn, I wish I smoked. But I can't get over the "it-kills-me" part of smoking.

Un-Perfect

July 14, 2000

My insomnia returned. I thought I kicked it, but apparently I didn't kick it hard enough. It's back.

Insomnia set in when I was in college. I simply never slept. I'd lie in bed all night staring at the clock, getting more and more anxious as time leaked forward, like a dripping faucet I couldn't fix. So annoying.

"Oh God, it's 2:30 a.m. If I go to sleep this instant, I'll get five hours of sleep. But there's no way I'll fall asleep right now because I'm still staring at the clock. Shit. Okay, I'll give myself thirty minutes to fall asleep. But then I'll only get four and a half hours of sleep! And it's Friday tomorrow, which means I'll be expected to party until 1:00 a.m. I'm never going to make it. What if I collapse at the bar due to sheer exhaustion and everyone thinks I'm drunk and they take me to rehab instead of my bedroom?"

Everyone was desperate to help me, so they would come with surefire remedies: Read a book, count backwards from one thousand, work out every day, drink excessive amounts of alcohol, have sex (that was Derek's), put lavender in my pillowcase, and take a bath before bed. The counting backwards idea would work, but as soon as I started to doze off and miss a number I would get excited and think, "It's really happening! I'm falling asleep! Oh. Shit. Not anymore. Why can't I sleep like a normal person!?"

It got so bad that when I went to bed my roommates said good luck instead of goodnight.

So being awake all night is not new and I'm kind of grateful that I have a mission throughout the night. At least I'm not just staring at a clock, I'm checking on a real, live human being to ensure her survival.

This makes me feel more normal than just lying there alone in the dark worrying about how my lack of sleep is going to ruin my life. I'd play out certain disasters like failing a test, getting into a car accident, and Derek breaking up with me because I was catatonic on a date. All because I didn't get a good night's rest.

There is something about the idea of everyone shutting down and not being aware of any harm that could come our way. It's spooky how everyone just descends into a state that is so close to death without a care in the world.

Anyway, while being an insomniac is not new to me, I still suffer for it. I cannot operate clearly. Conversations feel delayed and I don't respond appropriately, usually saying, "I'm sorry, what did you just say?" Or worse, I pretend I'm listening, agreeing with everything being said.

Last week, my mother-in-law cracked a joke about how Iowans don't have blinkers installed on their cars and I said, "Oh, really?" She said, "No. Not really. I was kidding because no one uses them." I looked at Derek horrified, asking him, "Wait, what did she just say???"

He laughed and nodded his head. "Classic Kelly."

He's right. That has happened more times than I can count. A lot of times he'll be talking to me and he'll say, "You're not even listening to me are you?" To which I reply, "What? Oh, no. I'm sorry. Okay, now what were you saying?"

Once a person has tapped out of a conversation, there's no getting it back. The answer is usually, "Forget it." Since I'm so tired, that isn't a problem.

Un-Perfect

July 16, 2000

I told my doctor how incredibly exhausted I am, so she ran a blood test on my thyroid.

She wants to put me on Synthroid. I don't want to go on medication. At least I don't think I do. I don't know. I don't know anything. I can't make a decision, which sucks because I used to love making decisions. I used to be smart.

Every day is overwhelming and today is no exception. Should I read a book or watch TV? Should I wear a sweatshirt or t-shirt? Should I take a nap or shower? Should I call my mom or write out Thank You cards?

Should I go on Synthroid or hope my body repairs itself?

What is Synthroid? I have a friend that had her thyroid burned off and now she has to live on it for the rest of her life. I don't want that.

What if my body becomes dependent on it and I can't live without it? I'm already on truckloads of allergy meds, so I really don't want extra stuff eroding my liver. Plus, the thyroid seems like kind of a big deal. Life and death hang in the balance of whether or not they can get the medication levels right.

Allergy medication is different. It's not a big deal if I miss a day. So what. I have a stuffy nose. But if I miss a

*day of thyroid medication, my body will rebel and I'll get
incredibly sick and possibly die.*

*My entire body is trying to re-adjust to losing the
human being that was stuffed inside of it. It's like picking
up a puzzle and throwing all the pieces in the air. It takes
time to put it back together.*

I'm going to wait and see if it's temporary. Besides, symptoms of thyroid dysfunction are being tired, depressed, hair falling out, and dry skin. Coincidentally, these are all symptoms of being a new mom.

Maybe the puzzle pieces are all just overlapping and will work themselves out. As my hormones start to settle into their appropriate levels, maybe my thyroid will follow suit and I'll be totally fine.

Who am I kidding, I can't handle all this shit.

I'm panicking that my body is breaking down because I can't get any rest. I'm having anxiety/allergy attacks almost every morning and night. How is everything supposed to find its way back when I haven't slept in weeks? And I cannot convince myself to take the thyroid medication.

I don't know why, I just don't want my body to get addicted to it and then I can't live without it. This scares me. I can't explain it, but I'm totally averse to going on that medication. It's just not right for me.

July 17, 2000

*Derek and I went to his work's golf tournament,
which required an overnight at Kim and Pete's house.*

Un-Perfect

The further we drove, the further I was away from Parker. I had a pit in my stomach and felt like I was going to barf with each passing mile. I hated that my daughter was so far away from me.

All I could think about was that my daughter knew I left her. I chose to leave her. I left my baby for an ENTIRE NIGHT. And nights are scary. She was probably scared to death and I wasn't there to comfort her.

Everyone kept saying, "You need time to yourself Kelly, so try and enjoy it." I wanted to throw a tantrum or get sick so I didn't have to go. I begged my body to get the flu so I wouldn't have to go, but nope, I stayed healthy and was forced to leave my daughter.

Even though I'm back home with her, it still makes me cringe knowing I left her. What mother leaves her 8-week-old daughter for more than 24 hours? At the very least, I want to slap everyone that encouraged me to leave her. It didn't feel right; it felt sadistic and mean. But of course I listened to everyone saying, "Kelly, you should enjoy some time for yourself." I didn't enjoy it, I feel sick with guilt for leaving my baby. Why do I listen to everyone else?

And the quiet car ride didn't give me peace like they said it would. It made me worry more. I focused on myself instead of Parker. I'm so selfish. I found myself looking out the car window on our three-hour drive thinking, "When I die, I'm going to miss trees and grass. I'm going to miss holding Derek's hand. I'm going to miss my daughter. My sweet, sweet daughter."

I don't know why I think I'm going to get sick and die, but I do. I worry that I have it too good. These thoughts are shelved when I'm dealing with Parker's screaming, so when it's quiet, I'm left worrying about my health.

So I was happy to pick up our little bundle of tantrum the following morning. I didn't care that she was screaming, I just wanted to bring her into my chest and keep her there and never, ever, ever leave her again. She makes me forget about myself and concentrate on someone else for a change.

When we picked her up, the bags were packed and waiting at the front door. Pete handed her over and said, "This is not normal. I've never experienced this much screaming in my entire life." *Out of all three of their children, not one of them was this much work?*

Pete said, "I don't know what we would have done if our kids screamed this much. I can tell you that everything else in your life is going to be a cakewalk. This is insane."

We had no idea it was that bad. Yes, we knew she was more work than other babies, but to frighten a father of three is a little extreme. And this is a man who doesn't get his feathers ruffled much, so we know this is not an exaggeration. My sister looked at me with pity and tried to give me a little hope. "Well, think of it this way, you're probably in the worst of it now and it will be gone in a month. I think colic only lasts for three months."

We drove home in shock. I said, "Did you realize it was as bad as it was?"

Derek said, "No, but it makes me feel better to know that we're at the end of our rope for a reason and we're not just being candy asses about it."

Un-Perfect

July 18, 2000

I'm reading a book where the character talks about all the simple things she loves. This inspires me to do the same. If I die, I want people to know what I loved.

So, let's see... I like the sound a pencil makes on paper when people write, I love trees, my husband has the greenest eyes I've ever seen, I like the sound of someone tapping on the computer, I remember the smell of my dad's old truck when I was little - it makes me feel safe. Chapstick reminds me of my mom, I love old pictures, clouds are amazing, the way my daughter smells/feels/sounds, the sound a droplet of water when it hits...anyway, I like being here.

And what if I left these things behind? I can't get my analytical head wrapped around this concept of "heaven". If there's a heaven and if the people in it are aware of the loved ones they can no longer hug, that would blow ass. Not my kind of heaven.

So let me get this straight: I get my wings and I play a harp on a cloud, but I'm forced to watch my daughter and husband from afar, unable to pierce that bubble of manifestation? I'd just "live" on the other side, screaming at an invisible wall. I'd be a ghost without a purpose, coasting around smoking a cigarette without the guilt of having it kill me, wondering what I'm supposed to do with eternity.

I probably *would* go around scaring little kids on Halloween because I'd be bored out of my mind. I'd stuff myself in their closets and move clothes around, pop out of the mirror when they're brushing their teeth and tickle their toes as they hop into bed.

How does a person in purgatory bide their time?

And there's no question that's where I'd be. Purgatory. Because I have difficulty making decisions. I can't even decide what to make for dinner tonight; tacos or spaghetti. How would I be expected to follow a blinding white light? Where does it go? Who is holding the flashlight? Is it just a decoy to see if I'd fall for a trick?

I need a lot of information before making a decision, especially of that magnitude. It's FOREVER. That's huge. I can't even commit to Playtex or Tampax. And why do they both end in "x"? Even Kotex. That is so weird. Did some genius determine that X marks the spot? Like, "insert here"? What the hell is that all about?

Anyway, I think God poured himself into these bodies, these tiny little containers, to see how we'd do. And what a shame that we bruise ourselves inside and out, not realizing that all the divine power is in us all along. I think we always seem to be waiting for something "up there" to wave a magic lightning bolt to fix us, when all that magic is sitting right inside our own heads.

The power of thought is crazy. Change your thoughts, change the world.

July 18, 2000

Had sex with D.

What if I never ever ever ever want to have sex again as long as I live? Is that bad?

Derek

7/18/00

YES!!!!!!!!!!!!!!!!!!!!!!!!!!!!!!!!!!!!

FINALLY had sex with my wife again after four months, two weeks and a few days.

We haven't been allowed to have sex since she was six months pregnant. That's a long dry spell.

Note: Secretly, I hope she doesn't lose all the baby weight. I'm crossing my fingers that about ten lbs stay on. I like how soft she is now, instead of being rail thin and hard bones on the edges. I think it's hot. She doesn't believe me, but it's true. Why do women think emaciated is sexy? Men like meat.

July 20, 2000

I went to ECFE (Early Childhood Family Education) today to meet some new moms, but it only made me feel more alone. I'm crying while I write this. I can't even see the stupid paper through my tears.

I sat in the circle with all the moms and their babies and Parker screamed THE ENTIRE TIME. Everyone kept looking at me like I was doing it wrong.

Maybe they're right. Maybe I am doing it wrong.
But I don't know what to do differently.

All the other babies were quiet or cooing and mine was screaming. So I got up to stand in the corner so the other moms could hear each other talk. I was about 20 feet from the circle yelling, "WAIT, CAN YOU REPEAT THAT? YOU MADE A NEW BROCCOLI DISH!? OH, THAT'S AWESOME!" I scream everything because no one can hear me over her shrieking. I was trying to keep a smile on my face, but it was coming undone. It was time to go before my mask eroded.

I reached down to get the bags I left under my seat, and Parker suddenly vomited, spewing formula everywhere. While she kept screaming, I got down on my knees trying to clean it up. I rocked her car seat with one hand, while cleaning up the puddle of barf with another.

I started crying. And no one reached out to help me. Not one. Unless you count the person who helpfully pointed out, "Your baby just barfed."

They just kept talking about how blessed they feel and how great their lives are. I am so lonely... trying to connect with someone that won't tell me, "Oh, you'll be fine." Or worse, have them look at my baby with wide eyes saying, "That's not normal, my baby never cries like that."

That's happened to me more times than I care to count. I'm NOT fine - and people are ignoring me when I tell them I'm overwhelmed. They keep saying that every new mother is overwhelmed and then they look at me like, "Why would you be an exception?"

Some people get downright annoyed when I try to describe how steamrolled I feel with this whole motherhood gig. One woman actually said, "Well, at some point, you'll just need to pull it together. That's what we all do."

I can't pull anything together because I'm suffocating under the words,

Un-Perfect

"I'm a bad mother." These words are like cement bricks... and the more they're repeated, the bigger and heavier they get. They bruise me inside and out.

I need someone to tell me they've been through this.

I need to hear their story so I can remind myself that I am a good mother. Somewhere in my head I know this to be true. I know I'm doing the best job I know how to do. But why isn't my best good enough? I love Parker so much and want to be the best mother for her. I look at all the other babies and think how lucky they are to have a good mom. Poor Parker got the bad mom. Me.

No one is confessing about how difficult this is. I don't get it - are they just pretending everything is peachy, or do they bottle up all the rage?

Or maybe it's simply not difficult for them and I'm an anomaly.

July 22, 2000

What causes colic? We figured out how to land a man on the moon, but we can't explain colic? That is bullshit.

I lay her in the crib because I'm afraid I will shake her. Plus, my body is weak and I don't have the strength to hold her anymore. I stare at her, this tiny baby flailing and thrashing in her crib, and wonder what she wants from me.

In fact, a few times I've yelled, "WHAT DO YOU WANT FROM ME!?" Then I feel bad that I yelled at her because she can't help it. No one can help it.

No one on this planet can help my daughter. She seems to be in excruciating pain, yet not one fucking doctor out there understands how to fix it.

Our society can fix broken arms, legs, and hearts, but we can't stop a baby from crying? That's ridiculous to me.

I can't help my daughter feel better. Isn't that what mothers are supposed to do? If she had Down Syndrome, I'd have a team of doctors and nurses to help me. Someone would define it for me and I'd understand what my role is. What is my role here? I feel like I have a hurricane attached to my hip all day and I can't control the weather to make it stop.

The definition for colic is, "A condition in which an otherwise healthy baby cries or screams frequently and for extended periods without any discernible reason." Oh really? That's what colic is? Wow, well mystery solved. Case closed. "No discernible reason." Guess that's it then.

That's the most worthless definition of anything I've ever seen.

July 25, 2000

I feel like a bad mom because I'm excited to go back to work in a couple of weeks. I love structure and routine. It feels safe. Expectations are like blinking beacons. "Wake up now. Drive your car. Balance this spreadsheet. Make dinner. Go to bed." Decisions are made for me and right now, that's a blessing because I can't decide on anything. Which brand of mascara, how much toilet paper to buy, if I want my mom to visit, what to wear… the list is endless.

Every decision is overwhelming. Where the hell did my brain go?

Un-Perfect

I was so opinionated and judgmental before I had Parker. To a fault, I know, but there's no preference for anything anymore. I was so brash and public with my thoughts, but now I seem to have handed over all intelligence to my daughter. I passed the torch to her and now I'm a meek, worthless, unintelligent, confused, woman.

I have nothing to wear to work, and we're not in a financial position to invest in a new wardrobe. Why is the fat from my hips pouring over the tops of my jeans like pudding? It's not like I'm storing milk there. I'm not a goddamn milk camel. I remove my jeans and panties and the words, "Victoria's Secret" are embedded into my skin like a branded cow.

But I get it. Eight point three pounds of Parker is worth fifteen pounds of muffin tops. I'm going to miss cuddling with her in the morning before the screaming begins. After work, I'll only get a couple hours with her and that will be during dinnertime, which I have deemed "The Witching Hour". It's not going to be quality time when she's howling and I'm kicking her bouncy seat while trying to not to burn pork chops. But we can't afford for me to stay home, so I have no choice.

And to be honest, the fewer choices I have, the better at this point.

I don't know if I could forgive myself for choosing to go back to work, even though I'm secretly excited to go back to something at which I excel. At least I used to be successful at it. Whatever brain I had left seems to be melting over this three-month leave from work. Lack of sleep has a way of eroding intelligence.

Derek

7/25/00

I almost had a heart attack a couple weeks ago when Kelly had one of her nightmares. She was screaming and even when she woke up and looked at me, she wasn't really looking at me. She just had this glazed look on her face.

Jesus Christ, going to sleep should be the easiest thing in the world, but she never stops thinking, worrying, considering, planning. Ever. I have never in my life heard screaming like that. It was like she was being attacked.

She's always talked in her sleep and sometimes even sleepwalked. I remember when we were first married and she walked out of the bedroom when I was watching TV in the living room. She just stood there staring at me. Scared the shit out of me.

My wife's energy level never comes down. She doesn't wake up like the rest of the world; she jumps out of bed, immediately talking about the day, having it all planned out before she finishes her first cup of coffee. As she rambles on about her To-Do List, I drink my Mountain Dew and watch ESPN. I can't take that much action right away in the morning.

I think we could both use some rest, but Kel won't take me up on my offers to take Parker for a drive or

Un-Perfect

play with her in the backyard while she sleeps. Screw it, I guess she'll just have nightmares then. I don't know what else to do other than offer help and have it rejected over and over again.

I'm beginning to think she doesn't trust me alone with Parker. Doesn't she think I'm a good dad? I carry Parks around in the football hold, bouncing up and down the stairs to stop the crying. My calves are killing me, but it works, so I do it. I bounce up and down fourteen stairs for hours until she falls asleep. Kelly could sleep then, but she doesn't. Instead she watches me from the living room and yaps about possible cures.

Her mom stopped over a few times and offered help, but Kel doesn't accept help from her either. And I don't think Judie's getting the full story about Parker. When she was over she said, "That's too bad Parker was having a rough night, but Kelly said things are better, so that's good."

Her mom thinks Parker had one rough night. For some reason, Kelly's not telling her own mother that it's all day and night, every day.

When I asked her why she doesn't have her mom help her, Kelly said, "Why tell my mom how bad it really is? She's just going to feel helpless because no one can fix this."

I think Kelly wants her family to think she has it all under control. She can't stand to have someone swoop down and "save" her and she knows that's what her sisters and mom will do if she fesses up about how hard this is for her.

I'm the only one who gets to witness her complaining, whining, and desperate schemes to cure colic. Her latest thing is only feeding her every four hours because she thinks she's over-feeding her, which is why she's spitting up.

Why can't she just accept that it's a tough gig that has no cure? Let it go already.

July 26, 2000

Beware of movies, sitcoms and even your neighbors, because what you see isn't real. There isn't a laugh track playing when you wake up at 4:30 a.m. to discover your child sleeping in puke. It's not cute when you yell at your husband for not doing his part and yell at him again for not doing it right.

When visitors stop in unannounced and you haven't showered for three days, it's not sweet - it's overwhelming. By the way, if you're used to instant gratification, you're in for a brutal slap in the face. Nothing is instant in motherhood

Un-Perfect

except the instant your baby is born and your label changes from "not mother" to "mother".

That is the only instantaneous part. Everything else is a slow evolution. You will never be one step ahead of the game, because your infant is now calling the shots.

Sleep comes at the mercy of your baby. If she's not sleeping, then neither are you. It's like walking into a cartoon, but it's not funny. I cry about once a week, which is huge for a woman that has cried maybe twice in her adult life.

I would be overjoyed if someone marched in my living room with a PowerPoint presentation, indicating the outcome of how Parker will work herself out of this colicky mess. I would see a direct correlation between the increase of her colic and my decrease in esteem.

"See here? This is where you started really showing your shitty tendencies as a mother. Right here. Do you see it? Right where her screaming takes a 90 degree angle upwards and your esteem nosedives into the ground."

I need to make motherhood more profitable for me, but I can't figure out how. If this was a business, I would enter variables into the presentation like timelines on bedtime, install naps, types of formula, levels of noise in the house, possible allergies, insert a calm mother instead of me, white noise or silence, rocking/bouncing vs. stillness...

I could go on and on and on. But I'm too tired to care.

Kelly Nordstrom

July 27, 2000

I'm held hostage in my home.

Why do people think I'm okay with my infant screaming at the top of her lungs? Do they think I enjoy 130 decibels in my ears all day long? When I bring her out, people think I'm an asshole for not doing something about it.

I need to get out of the house and enjoy fresh air and the sound of birds tweeting their non-judgmental songs of flight.

Flight. I wish I could take a flight somewhere. I don't even like to fly, but anything would be a welcome reprieve right now. Bring on the roaring engine, the ding-ding of someone wanting service and the drooling, snoring man dropping his sleeping, balding head on my shoulder.

I don't care if the plane bounces all over the sky with turbulence. Bring it on. As long as I don't have someone screaming at my face for twelve hours, I'm good.

Getting on the plane is the only time I welcome complete intoxication. Once I drank so much to nurse my anxiety, I fell flat on my face and promptly received an FAA warning. I don't even know what that is, but apparently it was very serious because they threatened to land the plane if I didn't shape up. I later received an email from a few new friends on the plane with pictures of me doing the "rocker sign" with my hands. The passengers in the background were not pleased.

But that is neither here nor there. Today, I'd behave myself if I could just get on a plane and escape for a few days. Maybe a week. Or two. I'd go

Un-Perfect

anywhere; even perform community service in a rice paddy somewhere. As long as no one is screaming in my face, it would be heaven. I could leave the Mommy Cult for a bit and remove myself from the scorn I feel when they give me the hairy eyeball. I bet no one would judge me in a rice paddy. I could wear that cool bamboo hat and help everyone apply sunscreen. I'd be appreciated and valued, instead of scorned and judged.

July 29, 2000

It was a bad idea. I knew it was, but I allowed myself to be conned into it anyway.

My sister Kim and I took all the kids to Chili's for lunch. As we ordered, I peeked into Parker's car seat and she was staring at me. Shit. She was awake.

I leaned across the booth to my sister, horrified, and said, "She's awake. What are we going to do? WHAT ARE WE GOING TO DO!" She said, "It will be fine, we'll take turns. Don't worry."

It wasn't fine. Parker started wailing at the top of her lungs. My nephew Ethan was so scared he pooped his pants and he's been potty trained for years. Everyone in the restaurant was staring at us wondering if I pinched her (I didn't, but secretly wanted to). So there I was again, back in that familiar place of everyone expecting me to fix the unfixable.

I know I ruined everyone's dining experience, but I hadn't seen the sun since May 19. I feel like a vampire. In fact, I look like one. My skin is chalky, I'm losing hair by the fistful and I never sleep. All I'm missing is the ugly trench coat.

So off we went. The sun-kissed goddess and the vampire grabbed their food in doggie bags and bolted out of there. I think I left a pile of hair in the booth during my anxiety-ridden exit.

Why is my hair falling out all the time? I have about seven hairs on my head and I'm trying to style it around the bald spots with no success. I'm like Hansel and Gretel, leaving little tufts of hair wherever I go in case I lose my way.

7/30/00 Sunday Muffins at Mom's

I sat at the counter today, finally confiding in my sisters and mom that I feel like a bad mom for wanting to go back to work because she screams all the time. They said, "What are you talking about, you're not a bad mom, Kelly. There is no such thing as a perfect mom." Well, there certainly is such a thing as a crappy mom. Because that's me.

Un-Perfect

What's crazy is that I can't stand being away from Parker. I feel like I'm going to barf as I drive to Target while D stays home with her. I can barely have her be in a different room in the house than me. I need her by me every minute of every day. Even at Muffins, I hate it when my niece takes her in another room, where I can't see her. Why does she do that? Why do people take her away from me all the time? I hear them laughing and singing, but it drives me crazy not being able to see my baby.

I can't stand it when people tell me I need a break. Who are these people that encourage a mother to leave her daughter? I need to be around her every second so I know nothing terrible is happening to her.

Derek's dad wants to take her to Marshall which is FOUR HOURS away. I can't allow her to go in a car without me. I can barely drive her myself without worrying about a car accident. I can't believe these people that want to take her away from me.

Maybe they see what a bad mom I am and they want to rescue her from me.

I want to stuff her back inside my body where she was always safe. Except for the umbilical cord wrapping around her neck which is what I worried about constantly when I was pregnant. God, is there no safe place for a child to be?

August 1, 2000

I'm so sleep deprived; I don't know what to do. Parker sleeps in 20 minute blocks throughout the day, and now with a sadistic twist, she's up every 1-2 hours through the night. I can't take it anymore. I'm finally sleeping in bits and pieces and now she's up. It seems we keep passing insomnia back and forth like a virus that won't go away.

I wish the sandman would show up at our house. I'd offer him a vodka tonic and have sex with him if it would get him to stay at our house longer.

The only relief I get is when Derek takes a feeding. I convince myself that it's healthy to un-hitch myself from her for a brief period of time.

Thank God I have a husband that is involved and wants to be involved. None of that crap from the 1950's where it's expected that I strap on an apron like a fucking straightjacket.

This morning I was sleeping so hard because Derek took the 5 am feeding. I slept from eleven to five. Heaven. It was the first big bulk of sleep

Un-Perfect

I've had since she was born. No, before she was born. I couldn't sleep even when I was pregnant because my hips ached as if they were disintegrating. No position was comfortable when trying to sleep with a bowling ball lodged above my pubic bones. It's just not a reality. But now, sleep is a beautiful thing and I was enjoying six full un-interrupted hours of it.

Until he brought her into bed with us.

I just about killed him. Why would he think that's a good idea? "Hmmmm…sleeping new mom, bring squawking baby into bed." Yeah, that makes great sense. How on earth did he come to this conclusion? I heard him whispering to her, "Should we snuggle in with Mommy? Huh? Do you want to see Mommy?"

No, imbecile, she doesn't want to see Mommy. Every time she sees Mommy, she screams. It's not a difficult formula to compute. Mommy makes Parker cry.

So of course they get into bed and 10 minutes later, she starts squirming, then she opens her eyes and sees me and immediately starts bawling. I realize I look like a scary clown in the morning, but isn't love supposed to be blind?

So while everyone else in the world was sleeping soundly, we were scrambling to calm a storm. I'm getting tired of trying to find myself in the wake of these storms. Every night, after it finally comes to an end, I'm left searching for pieces of myself.

I dig around in the rubble, finding things I thought were long gone. "Oh - strength and courage - there you are! I thought I lost you forever from that last round of storms." I hold them tight to my chest because I need them for the solidity of my home. My being. Hopelessness has a way of seeping in through the wood, like termites, when strength and courage are lost.

But little treasures like laughter, esteem, confidence, and joy get tossed around quite a bit. These are luxuries, like jewels. Some days they're shattered into dust like a house in a tornado. Sometimes it takes days, maybe a week, to get them back together into their beautiful, brilliant, shiny form. Laughter has gone missing for a while. I long for the day when I hold it in my hands, never letting it go again. I love to laugh. I miss it.

Derek

8/3/00 2:34 A.M.

Why the hell won't our kid sleep?

Every other kid goes to sleep until morning. Ours never sleeps. EVER.

She used to sleep okay through the night and all of a sudden she's not happy day or night. Nothing in the routine changed. Kelly hasn't even gone back to work yet, which by the way, makes me feel guilty. She doesn't have a choice and that sucks. I feel shitty.

But on the other hand, I want to be there for Parker. I want to be at all of her games when she's older, I want to eat dinner with my family every night, I want to be there. I don't want to be a "ghost dad" away on business trips all the time, missing out on my life.

I remember hearing about the slutty girls in high school or in college and it never fails, their dads were

Un-Perfect

deadbeats. I don't want my daughter walking around with low self-esteem and having all those high school wolves preying on her. No way. Plus, it's what I'm here for. I'm here to be Parker's dad, not just some guy hanging around on the edges of her life, paying the bills.

Shit, my alarm is going off in four hours and I'll have to go to work. I will be driving under the influence of no rest. Again. I feel drunk, but I haven't had a beer in months. Lately, I've been swerving my car all over the road because when I blink, my eyes want to stay shut. Lack of sleep can actually be more hazardous to people on the road than a three-martini lunch.

Note: I'm too tired to have sex.

August 4, 2000

We had another Well Visit. The pediatrician said he has never seen colic this severe. He just leaned toward us and said, "I'm sorry, I don't know what I can offer you. I've never seen a case this severe."

What the hell? Aren't doctors supposed to know everything?

I'm relieved to know that I'm not being a pansy about how exhausting this is. I also feel crappy because apparently I've created the crabbiest human being on the planet.

As we left the doctor's office, a mom in the waiting room said, "Oh, shot day? Poor baby." I screamed over the crying, "NO. NOT SHOT DAY! SHE'S COLICKY". I pointed at Parker's wailing face and yelled, "ALWAYS LIKE THIS. ALL DAY!"

I just walked out. I don't need another look of pity. Every day I have a pity party for myself. I'm the only one invited because no one else wants to celebrate with me.

I don't care.

The other day I was talking to the walls and said, "I feel so sorry for myself." They just stared at me. Bright yellow "sunshiny" walls. Happy walls. That's why I painted them yellow. Because they make me feel happy and bright. Now they mock me, reminding me of who I used to be.

If I had the energy, I'd paint them black.

After explaining the rare severity of her colic, the pediatrician asked for our permission to be a helpline for other parents of colicky babies. He wants there to be support for parents of colicky babies. I'm sure this newfound need is

Un-Perfect

coming from listening to me complain about how lonely I am and how people avoid me like the plague.

The plan is that when her colic subsides (if it ever subsides), he will give our number to struggling parents. I'm happy to do it. Helping someone else feel less lonely will make me feel really good. But I'm a little leery. I'm not seeing any other babies screaming like ours, so I'm feeling once again like we're the only ones dealing with colic. Unless all the other parents are hiding out in their homes, waiting for the storm to pass.

August 8, 2000

Today was my first day back at work. Yes, my clothes were way too tight, I'm balding and have black circles under my eyes, but I'm happy. I have a purpose again. People are happy to see me. I have a job in which I can excel and no one is screaming at my face.

Everyone knows how to burp themselves. No one barfed on me after lunch. I didn't have to wipe anyone's poopy ass in the bathroom. I walked through the halls without bouncing anyone on my hip saying, "It's okay, it's okay."

It was heaven. Never mind that I have no idea what I'm supposed to be doing for my actual job, I don't really care about that part. I'm a member of a community again. I have a posse of friends that aren't worried they'll "catch" colic. People can hear what I'm saying because I'm not trying to speak over ear-ringing screams. They see me. I exist again.

I picked Parker up from Peggy's daycare at four o'clock and Peggy looked a little tired. I opened the door to find Parker screaming in the Baby Bjorn attached to Peggy's chest.

She yelled, "DOES SHE HAVE GAS? BECAUSE I'VE NEVER HAD A BABY CRY THIS MUCH IN 24 YEARS!"

No gas, just colic, Peggy.

I cannot imagine how she did it with six other kids in the daycare. One of Parker is equivalent to all six. She could out-scream all of them. It's a miracle that Peggy made two meals and a snack with a screaming infant strapped to her body.

It would be like running a triathlon with sandbags fastened to your body. And then add a pair of headphones playing loud static. This would affect anyone's performance. Poor Peggy. I feel bad, but not bad enough to pull Parker out of daycare.

It is the first time I've felt any kind of hope. Someone cares. Someone is willing to link arms with me. Derek has been amazing, but I need someone with Peggy's experience to understand that this too shall pass. D and I are amateurs needing someone to help point us in the right direction.

Peggy has never had a baby cry this much, but I know she'll stay by me until the storm is over. There is simply something comforting and peaceful about

Un-Perfect

this woman who is quickly becoming my savior. And it's only been one day. But I know that she is supposed to be in our lives to help us. I could cry thinking about it.

My mother and sisters have been a strong net for me, but they can only be there as much as I allow them. I don't understand why I can't admit to them the failure I've become. I don't want them to see the real me: Vulnerable, scared, confused, and sad.

I'd be so pissed if a friend, sister or my mom knocked on my front door saying, "I'm here to take Parker for a couple hours to help you out. You get some rest." This is what I would hear: "I'm here to rescue your daughter because you suck at motherhood. You're a bad mom and since I'm a better mom than you, I'm here to save the day." It irritates me just thinking about it.

I've groomed them to believe that I'm strong, independent and have my life together. I'm quite fond of that label. If they think I'm okay, then maybe I'm going to be okay. If people aren't treating me like a fragile insect, then I can pretend that indeed I really am as strong as they think I am. I need to have people believing in me because right now, I don't.

So that leads me to Peggy. She's only known me as a new mother. I'm real with her because I don't have the energy to pretend to be anyone else. I'm grateful for this reprieve of acting to be a picture of strength and sobriety. I've been so alone and now here she is, a woman willing to partner with me. She's on my team and will see it through because she is that kind of woman. Strong. And I need strength.

August 9, 2000

There are a few other women at work that returned from maternity leave within the last couple of weeks. They're all crying at their desks explaining to me how much they miss their baby and how hard it is to leave him/her.

I don't feel this way at all.

Which way is normal? Am I being a cold bitch or are they just sappy? Why am I not crying at my desk like they are?

But I'm the one pretending to be like them, which means they're right and I'm wrong. Something is wrong with me.

But as much as I appreciate a break from the screaming, I do feel heartache. Handing my sweet girl over to the arms of another woman, no matter how great, is disheartening. Peggy will be able to touch the golden curls of Parker's hair anytime during the day and I cannot. I cannot reach out and touch her chubby cheeks for eight hours. But the reprieve from survival mode trumps my feelings of missing her. I need this break for my sanity.

I also feel heartache for failing. I've been home for three months and could not make my daughter happy. Not in three months of connecting with her 24/7. Why couldn't I learn her needs in ninety days? Some mothers brag about having instinct and knowing what their child needs before the child even knows they need it. Apparently, I'm missing the maternal instinct and I want to feel it, understand it, and know what my child needs.

I was watching Animal Planet the other day and even a fucking monkey has maternal instinct. Why am I so defective? I came with broken parts and they weren't discovered until I gave birth. It's like realizing a car doesn't have heat until winter hits and there's no warmth to give. No one in the car feels safe and comfortable.

Un-Perfect

It's hard to admit this, but Parker is better off with Peggy than with me, her own mother. Peggy is calm and centered. Parker seems to be calmer at daycare, surrounded by six other rambunctious children, than in the quiet of her own home.

August 12, 2000

Derek and I recorded the hairdryer because white noise seems to help. I can only blow-dry my hair for so long. I've even left it on, just laying it on the floor next to her bouncy seat, but then I worried it could start her seat on fire. So I turned it off.

D and I play the tape on the highest volume, hoping to sedate her with a cloud of noisy confusion. It worked for about twenty minutes, but then she discovered the trick and was back to piss and vinegar. She's so smart.

The vacuum is a godsend and we've been using that for a while, until we burned a hole in the carpet. We had it tipped up so it wasn't actually on the carpet, but I think we were so grateful she was sleeping during the day that we fell asleep as well.

I have no idea how long it was frying the carpet, but it was long enough to create a bald spot resembling the back of my head.

This is getting dangerous, trying to find white noise that works. I heard one couple runs the bathwater to create that sacred white noise. No one is in the bathtub, but it still seems not only a little dangerous, but environmentally unsound.

I wish there was a "Welcome Colic" basket, complete with headphones, ear plugs, a memoir of other parents that survived this hell, headset for the TV and phone, shitloads of batteries for the vibrating bouncy seat. A bonus in the basket would be baby-safe headphones featuring white noise.

This basket does not exist.

I want to know that I'm not sending my daughter straight to a therapist's couch in the future. I can just see her now smoking a cigarette, explaining what a number I did on her. "Well, it started with my idiot mother who couldn't handle a few tears and totally abandoned me. So I'm on meth to protect myself from the pain because obviously, if I cry, she freaks, so I live my life totally numbed out on whatever mind-numbing goodies I can inject, ingest and shoot.."

August 27, 2000

Last week was hell. She was up every two hours. This does not mean I'm getting two hours of sleep. Having her up every two hours translates into feeding, burping, changing jammies with spit up, changing her diaper, singing back to sleep, then finally falling to sleep and then she's up again.

So I'm not actually getting a bulk of two hours of sleep. That would be literally, a dream. I'm getting about

Un-Perfect

twenty minutes. Max.

That's enough for my eyelids to scrape over my eyeballs like sand-filled curtains, and then boom, each little whimper pulls back the curtains back again.

I find myself falling asleep while standing. What am I, a cow? I'm afraid drunk teenagers are going to break into my house and start "Kelly Tipping".

When I'm in a meeting I stare at the speaker, unable to move a muscle or respond in any way, shape or form. My mouth was even hanging open during an especially boring topic of advertising legalese. If it's possible, I'm learning how to sleep with my eyes open, pretending to work.

Last night Derek finally got her to sleep on his chest around 4:00 a.m. This is after we passed her back and forth like a football, each of us collapsing onto the sofa during our time out. Then we started the argument of, "Well I have to go to work too" and debated which job is more important.

We figured since he makes double my salary, his job is more important. But since I'm such a whiny bitch without sleep, he'll take the last shift and try to drag it out on the couch. He succeeded, which probably explains why he'll always bring home more bacon than me. I just don't have the tenacity to see things through when I'm tired and doing a less-than-stellar job. If I'm failing, I want to quit. If I can't do it perfectly, then I don't want to do it at all. He, on the other hand, doesn't seem to fail at anything, so I passed the parental torch to him around 3:00 a.m. and called it a day.

He's the perfect one in this marriage, trumping me in the Parental

Showdown. I'm just the sham pretending to be immaculate. I'm jealous. This parenting gig is coming so natural to him and I'm the dithering idiot trying to figure out how to put one foot in front of the other.

His alarm went off at 5:00 a.m., so I woke him from the couch. The horror on his face when I said, "Your alarm went off. It's time to go to work" was priceless. He was slapping my hand away from his shoulder as if I was an annoying mosquito. I whispered, "Honey, it's time to go to work. Honey. HONEY! GET UP!" He muttered, "fucking bullshit" while raking his hands through his hair on his way to the shower. He's so good looking with a five o'clock shadow, messy hair and pajama pants that hang low on his hips. He even has beautiful feet.

I stayed awake and fed her, enjoying a rather unusual peace. She must have deflated her lungs last night. Nothing seems to be left in those little balloons today. While it was a peaceful beginning, I still couldn't help being whiney about how tired I was and explained to everyone in the office, detail by excruciating detail, my night last night.

I even belted out in a meeting, "Well what did YOU do last night? Play *video games*? I was up all night with a screaming infant." This isn't actually true, since I made the last baby pass around 3:00 a.m., but I was looking to score some sympathy votes. But I should know better. The advertising industry is not the place to score sympathy votes. This industry seems to be filled with 24-year-olds dressed in swanky clothes, pulsating with hormones trying to get each other in the sack. It's either the Sexy Young People or The Sobbing Mothers (the few working mothers sobbing at their desks because they miss their babies so much). I don't relate to either group, so I sit in my cube with black circles weighing down my eye sockets like horseshoes.

Will I ever feel normal again? I'm feeling left out in the cold here, looking into the warm cabin on a snowy day, not being invited in for hot

Un-Perfect

chocolate. I can see all the smiling faces and hear all the laughter, but I'm not part of it. It's all happening through the frosty windows and I'm on the outside, wishing someone would see me and wave me inside.

DEREK

8/30/00 4:00 A.M.

We were passing Parker off back and forth while we each took a few hours through the night. I was on my shift, bouncing Parker up and down and pacing back and forth by the stairs. Suddenly Kelly came out of the bedroom and gave me a look of hatred that said, "What the hell are you doing?" In fact she actually said that.

I looked at her and shrugged my shoulders like, "What do you want? Speak!" Parker was ALMOST asleep, dammit. Kelly said, "Do you think you could walk her in the basement so the screaming is not right outside of the bedroom door?"

I'm doing the best I can do, trying to drink a Mountain Dew while cradling Parker in the football hold. And yes, I can walk her around in the basement, but I like to feel a little normal walking on carpet instead of the freezing cement floor in my bare feet. Christ.

Kelly Nordstrom

When it's my turn it's never good enough. There's always a slightly better way that only Kelly knows about. "Bounce her like this, feed her like this, pat her back like this…"

To all the mothers out there who do everything better, I say: Appreciate the fact that your husband is trying. We are doing our best.

We didn't play with dolls when we were growing up. We didn't babysit infants. This is kind of a first round draft for us, and we're doing the best we know how to do.

Give us a fucking break with that "you're-doing-it-wrong" look. There's no need to exhale while we fumble with our babies, shifting from one arm to another. And we don't need to be reprimanded by you when we do it.

We know that moving a sleeping baby is like igniting a grenade. We get it. And sometimes we still choose to do it and if the screaming starts, we'll deal with it. Holding a sleeping baby on one arm for two hours can hurt. The arm can fall asleep and get all tingly, our elbow might cramp up, we might need to get up to take a piss.

The point is, shit happens and we wake the baby. We don't need to see your head bang back and forth like we're clueless idiots.

Un-Perfect

September 2, 2000

*D and I drop into bed at 10:30 like lead weights,
usually in a fight because we're so frustrated with all the
screaming.*

*A year ago we'd share an hour of pillow talk,
touching each other's faces and laughing. Now we barely
mumble "G'night." Where did our connection go? It's like
someone shuffled the deck of cards and lost the king and
queen of hearts.*

*I remember telling him I was pregnant and his
hands went up to his face instinctively in shock. Protecting
himself. Maybe he knew all along what was coming and I
was naïve to think having a baby would evolve our marriage
into something even better.*

*It's not like we were limping along needing cardiac
paddles to resuscitate our marriage. We were happy. We
laughed. But something was missing. After four years, we
wanted a baby and we wanted one bad. We tried for almost
a year, each month painting failure in red. The signal of
debt.*

*Apparently, my body wasn't the reservoir of fertility
as I thought it was. I was beginning to resent every person*

that walked the stores with kids. Why do they get those and I don't? I was like a whining toddler trying to grab candy on the way out of the convenience store. "No, you can't have a baby. You know better than that. Your body sucks."

But we continued with our valiant efforts in the sack. Sex was more like making a deposit at the bank, rather than love and faith. But we did it. After almost a year, a second pink line showed up like a new road being paved. I gladly picked up my car and placed it on the new road. Derek wasn't as quick. He walked the halls in a daze for about three days.

One morning I asked, "Did you see a different person in the mirror this morning?" He said, "Yeah, I can't believe someone's dad was looking back at me. I'm going to be someone's DAD. That's HUGE."

And now he's the one shining through on the parental front. It's always been easy for him. You always know the person you're going to marry. You know their strengths and weaknesses. But you don't know what kind of parent they will be. I'm lucky that he's a good one.

I wonder what he thinks of me? I can't possibly be the mother he thought I would be. I cannot get my life together. I'm always falling apart and complaining about how tired I am.

But we wanted this together and I'm still so happy with our decision even though I'm a bumbling idiot. We wanted to look into our children's eyes and see generations of those before us, floating in the blue and green speckles of their eyes. We wanted to create forever. We wanted to smile a sleepy smile in the morning when our baby was snuggled between us, still sleeping.

A few of these dreams are happening, but sleeping is not one of them. We've worked so hard to build a solid foundation and she keeps chipping away at

Un-Perfect

it with her secret, diabolical hammer. Then we have to add more concrete and pick up everything she smashed and start again. Over and over again. We rebuild our marriage every day and if we skip one because we're too tired to connect, we fall behind and the marriage starts to suffer.

I can't imagine what would happen if we didn't build that foundation for four years before having a baby. What would be left to hold on to? What memories would there be to tether each other to the beautiful things that aren't happening at that moment? How could a person understand that their partner is simply taking a sabbatical from their beautiful self and will be back at a later date? If that foundation wasn't there, how could you trust that they'll be back?

I have to believe this experience would blow any marriage apart that didn't have beams made of steel. It's impossible to switch to survival mode if survival mode is all there is. There has to be more to the foundation than just surviving.

A reservoir of good memories, ones complete with trust and faith and happiness is a good thing to have tucked into your back pocket. So when you're running low, you can reach into your pocket, grab one out, and say, "Oh, that's right! He was there for me when I had my wisdom teeth pulled out all those years ago. He almost fainted, but he was there with a balloon and a smile until he had to lie down next to me."

Little reminders keep you tethered together like a string of Christmas lights. Coping is dealing with stress in a way that prevents you from freaking out. Sometimes you need to look over and make sure the other blinking light is working so you can take a break. It's hard being bright all the time.

The psychological definition of coping is "the process of managing taxing circumstances, expending effort to solve personal and interpersonal problems, and seeking to master, minimize, reduce or tolerate stress or conflict." My pockets of memories help me cope.

September 12, 2000

I've hit my all-time low. As if I wasn't already sinking in the ugly boat, I now can't wear contacts because I've developed an allergy to the solution. My eyes turn blood-red if I try to wear them.

I already looked like a vampire, but now I'd actually scare little children. Every day would be Halloween for me with this pasty skin, balding head, black circles, and now what appears to be bleeding eyes. I think people are beginning to wonder if I'm a meth addict and try to catch me shooting up over the lunch hour.

My thick glasses magnify the black circles under my red, swollen eyes. These half-moons are hovering like dirty socks taped under my sockets.

With a prescription of 20/600, my spectacles are quite a spectacle. They are like a couple of water glasses strapped to my head. Then I get the jokes all day. "Can you even SEE through those things?" or "What the hell is on your face?"

When I got contacts, I no longer had to wear this contraption in public, which means I haven't worn them outside of my home since 1987. But now here they are in all their glory. On my face. In public.

Un-Perfect

I thought getting a new hairdo would numb the pain of the glasses, but it only made it worse. I went to my beloved gay stylist who said I would be *so fabulous* in short, blonde hair. After shaving my hair like a landscaping tree and dying it bright blonde, I was indeed transformed.

Into what, I'm not sure.

I screamed at the mirror, realizing there was nothing I could do. All my beautiful brown curls were dead at my feet. Tombstones of younger, better, sexier days. I left the house with long brown curly hair and returned looking like an Amish person with a mullet. Why did I think this would be a good decision? I should not be making any decisions. Ever. I'm always wrong.

Derek was sucker punched. I walked in the house and he slapped his hands up over his mouth and just stared. Blank. I stood there looking like a psychotic lawn gnome. All I could say was, "Yeah." He stared at me the entire night. Watching me pour Lucky Charms into a bowl, watching me brush my teeth, watching me watch TV, watching me play with Parker.

I guess that was his way of diluting the shock, like aversion therapy. Make yourself stare at it to desensitize your reaction. The thing is, I have a few weddings coming up and I'm going to need to over-drink at their receptions to make myself look better... to myself. It's a shame when you have to wear your own beer goggles.

It could be worse. I could be wearing it with my headgear like I did in 1987. I didn't have the "cool" headgear, if there is such a thing. Instead, mine was kind of a hat/helmet. This contraption was strapped to the top of my head like it was keeping my jaw from falling off my face. My own mother said, "Actually, I can't let you wear that to school anymore. It's just... you can't." She knows social suicide when she sees it.

DEREK

9/12/00

No comment on the haircut. That is like asking "Do these jeans make my butt look big?" Any man with a brain knows to plead the fifth to questions like that. No way, I'm not talking about the new hairdo.

9/17/00 Sunday Muffins At Moms

"Hellooooo!"   I walked into the Grand Entrance to reveal myself to everyone at the counter. My goggles, mullet and me. Mom is immediately at the door ready with a hug, which makes me feel so good I want to cry. She says, "Wow, I haven't seen those glasses in a while!"

I explain that out of nowhere I am now allergic to my contact solution. This of course invites a round of heckling from everyone, which I would normally have fun with, but when I'm not sleeping, not much is funny.

My brothers-in-law said, "Holy SHIT! Are you legally blind - seriously, are you?" It's mortifying to be yet again, the ugly one in the room. I'm sure they're thanking their

Un-Perfect

lucky stars they married the good-looking Rasmussen girls instead of me.

I asked Dad, "What do you think of these specs, Dad?" He said, "Well Loveface, I say if you can see out of them, then I think they're a good thing. You want mushrooms in your omelet?"

I sat at the counter looking nothing like my beautiful sisters with my goggles strapped to my face. The song, "One Of These Things Is Not Like The Other" kept playing over and over again in my head.

I already felt lower than low when I was alone looking in the mirror at home, but now when I sit next to The Beautiful People, it's apparent that I wasn't beating myself as much as I should have been.

My sisters don't see it. They explain that my hair is not that bad while Derek stands on the sidelines raising his eyebrows to convey, "Are you serious? You're condoning this haircut?" But here's the catch: While they say it's not that bad, it's understood that they *themselves* would never get it cut like this.

Isn't that like saying a hideous bridesmaid dress is fine on *you,* but they wouldn't be caught dead in it?

September 25, 2000

It seemed like such a great idea.

Derek and I would walk in the 10k run/walk event with Parker strapped to our backs like we were true hikers. Six miles of in-depth conversation, laughing, and losing that extra 10 lbs.

I pictured rock solid abs and sun-kissed highlights in my hair by the time I crossed the finish line. I was pumped. In my delusional head, I thought 6.2 miles would be nothing more than a leisurely stroll. Anything was possible after pushing a human being out of my crotch. How could anything match the physical endeavor of labor and delivery?

To say that we were unprepared is an intense understatement.

I wore jeans with Keds on my feet. Derek wore flip flops. I glanced around at the start line and we looked like hung over losers compared to the horses at the gate.

These runners were serious. It was too late to turn back. The gun went off and we started walking. Everyone took off like rockets and we were left strolling in Keds and flip flips.

People were cheering, "You can do it!"

Derek glared at me and said, "You've got to be

Un-Perfect

fucking kidding me."

Mile 2: blisters on our feet.

Mile 3: hopelessness of never finishing.

Mile 4: blood on our backs from the backpack filled with a sleeping child.

Mile 5: screaming at each other at the tops of our lungs.

Mile 6: the "cone cart" driving 2 feet behind us picking up the race cones.

Finish: considering that if we can't walk 6.2 miles together, we may as well sign divorce papers.

We were debating (yelling) with each other, trying to consider who was the bigger idiot. Was it me for suggesting this event? Or him for agreeing to it? If we were that stupid, how are we going to raise a child?

I was even pissed at Parker. I almost woke her up and said, "Listen you little prick, it's time you get out of that backpack and carry your own weight around here." But we made it. After about 3 hours of blood, sweat and tears, we crossed the finish line.

We will never do that again. Ever.

DEREK

10/1/00

Now I understand why the FBI uses sleep deprivation as a torture tactic. I'm surviving on

Mountain Dew. I feel sick to my stomach.

Kelly looks the same as me. Brutal.

Are her glasses hideous? Hell yeah. Do I care? No.

She always asks me if I second-guess myself or if I feel like a bad dad because Parker cries so much. The answer is no. I feel like a good dad that is taking care of a cranky infant. Big deal.

I don't think I'm causing Parker's pain, but Kelly takes it personally, like Parker is choosing to make her feel bad.

No matter how many times I tell her that Parker loves her and she's a good mom, she sits at the kitchen counter saying, "I don't know, I just feel like I'm screwing it all up, otherwise she'd be happy." C'mon, Kelly became a *mother* not a doctor. Hell, even our doctor couldn't cure colic.

Shit happens. So what. Parker is colicky. Could be worse. Let's move on.

Note: I want the confident Kelly back.

October 3, 2000

At our last Well Visit, the doctor-that-can't-cure-colic was concerned that Parker has torticollis, a condition that shapes her head wrong. He suspects it's the way she was

Un-Perfect

positioned in my belly when I was pregnant with her.

Yet another thing I've done wrong. How can I carry a fetus wrong? Even a kangaroo understands how to carry a baby in her pouch.

Anyway, we went to physical therapy a few times to learn some exercises for her neck. She's crying a lot less, so I'm guessing that was the cause of her wailing. I'd scream too if my neck hurt.

If we didn't do the physical therapy, she would need a helmet to correct the shape of her head. Personally, I thought it would have been a nice safety precaution. Derek didn't agree.

Since the screaming is less, I thought it would be a great time to take care of this "keeping-me-awake-all-night" business. I cannot be the parent I need to be when I'm dragging on fragments of sleep. It feels like I hang onto these pieces of sleep throughout the day, dragging them like lead weights around my ankles.

Derek was in Vegas, so I let her cry it out at bedtime and trusted that she would settle herself throughout the night. I called the nurse line and made her stay on the phone with me. For a while we just sat there, she and I, listening to each other breathe with my daughter screaming in the background. I just needed someone on the other line that was thinking clearly, because lately, I'm feeling like a lobotomy patient. I simply cannot think straight. I needed her to help me stay confident with my decision.

Yesterday I put my thong on sideways *and* inside out. The ass floss was cutting into my personal parts. How unfortunate that it took all day to realize it.

So I needed to do this before I actually start wearing underwear on the outside of my clothes. Or forget to put on clothes altogether. I also needed someone to persuade me to believe that I wasn't a bitch for having Parker cry it out. I felt so cold and uncaring. Don't Native Americans all live together forever? If it takes a village, why am I sitting alone with a stranger, a nurse, on the other end of a telephone? Maybe it's not so bad to just have Parker sleep with us until she's 18 years old. Maybe that's not such a bad idea. Maybe we cou… quiet.

Peace and quiet at 8:30 p.m.

It only took twenty minutes and I just freed up my evenings to watch bad TV, talk on the phone, paint my toenails, do laundry, shower…anything I want! ANYTHING! I had time for myself again! I did it! I closed my eyes, smiled and pumped my fists in the air as if I just won a gold medal. I celebrated by having Oreos and reading People Magazine. It was heaven.

October 6, 2000

Derek returned from Vegas and while he knew I was successful at the crying-it-out deal, he still didn't want to be a part of it. I told him he can't un-do the work I did because it was difficult enough doing it the first time. Plus, to unravel all the work Parker had done would be confusing to her.

I begged him, "Just wait it out, she's sleeping through the night now. It only takes twenty minutes." So we

Un-Perfect

put her to bed at 8:15 and by 8:17 he was crying. At 8:20 he tried going into her bedroom to get her and I braced my arms across the doorframe, so he couldn't go in and get her.

He was livid and said I was a cold-hearted bitch. This didn't sit well with me since I thought the very same thing the first night I did this. But I held strong. He was not going in there. I earned the right to have a couple free hours in the evening. It felt so good to make a solid decision again.

He said I was barbaric and if I planned on making him listen to his daughter cry again the next night, he will be getting a hotel room. The luggage came out, but by the time he got socks in there, it was quiet. We made it. And we made it through the entire night. Our very first eight-hour night's sleep as a family in our own respective beds.

In the morning, we woke up together for the first time since we had our daughter. Our noses were touching, breathing each other in. I woke up before he did and watched him sleep. He has the longest eyelashes I've ever seen. Parker has his eyelashes. And his eyebrows – they're perfect. Parker has his eyebrows. I like it when his hair gets too long and curls behind his ears. Behind those eyelids are the greenest eyes in the world. I've never seen a color like that. Parker's eyes turn that color when she wears green. They're always bright blue - my blue - until she wears green. It's like she's a chameleon paying respects to each of us. I love that she looks like Derek. It's the big, wide, bright eyes that resemble him. Derek doesn't see it, but I do and I love it. I love that she looks like her daddy. It's just so sweet.

Kelly Nordstrom

Our marriage ran out of gas, stumbled off the tracks, and blew all the tires on the sharp rocky road. There was no other way for us to survive the screaming without sacrificing the quality of our marriage. Survival is defined as "continued existence after hardship or adversity; to remain alive." We are alive.

I have a feeling this will be a new chapter in our marriage. The old marriage, sans children, was finished with the words, "I'm pregnant." Those two words gently closed the book on our first phase of marriage.

I have no idea how many phases there are in a marriage, but I do know the feeling of a chapter closing. It feels like walking through a door and only when it closes, do you realize you can never go back. The life as you know it is now broken into vivid memories, only to have the spotlight when called upon by you. Otherwise, all the experiences sit quietly on a shelf until one day; you dust them off and bask in them for a while.

We are the only species that are blessed with the awareness of our own existence. To be aware of time passing by with each kiss, hug, thought, and tear. This has always been a significant concept to me, even as a five-year-old. I was lying in bed one night when I created a concept of numbered breaths. What if God only gave each of us a certain number of breaths and we don't know when we'll run out? What if he only gave me five thousand? I started counting my breaths, which got increasingly fast, and when I got up to one hundred, I was almost hyperventilating.

I leaned over and whispered to my sister, "Kim? KIM! I think I'm dying. I think I'm running out of breaths! What do I do?!" She let out a big sigh, totally annoyed with my hysterics. "Go tell Mom and Dad."

I wish that was the resolution for everything. But now here's a twist. I'm the mom and Derek is the dad. I don't have answers for hyperventilating children. I don't know trigonometry. I don't know why lightening doesn't strike high-rise apartment buildings in the middle of a city.

Un-Perfect

But I do I know that if I waited to have all the answers, I would never have become a mother. Life doesn't work that way. It works well for a bank account. You have all the facts and you make a decision. For example, buying designer jeans when you have fifty dollars in your account is not a good idea. Trust me, I know. My bank knows too.

But deciding to become a mother is a decision from the heart. There are no answers, facts, or guarantees, yet so many of us take that leap of faith because our soul has a need to create and love. I can Google facts. You can teach me geography. I can learn those things. They can be taught.

What cannot be taught is compassion, love, motivation, perseverance, and acceptance. These things are born from the heart. *Life* teaches us these things, not a spreadsheet or map. So it's okay to not have answers. In fact, it's preferred. That way, life can open up its arms and teach us new things that we are ready to learn. And only when we're ready, will we actually be aware of the lesson.

Perspective is so much better when a body is rested. I can honor and appreciate my life. I feel like I can look back on the colic ordeal instead of reacting to it. We made it. We really made it.

October 12, 2000

Sometimes, when I am holding Parker, people will walk up and say "Oh, look how cute you are! I just want to take you home with me! Do you want to come home with me?"

To me, this is not funny or cute… it just reminds me that there are people out there who kidnap children.

Just the other day I was at Target and Parker was in the Bjorn. A man came up and asked to take a picture of us because he hasn't seen this in his country and wants to develop and sell it when he returns home.

"Sure!" We smiled for the camera and went on our way. But now - now I think he's after me and probably stalking us so he can steal Parker from me. A stranger has a picture of my daughter and me. Why didn't I protect us and say no? Why don't I have a maternal, protective instinct?

I find myself looking at people now when I run errands with Parker. The grocery store is the worst. I REALLY hate having to return the cart to the corral after I load up my groceries. I feel like a kidnapper is watching and waiting for me to leave Parker alone in her car seat so they can steal her from me.

So I just leave the cart in the lot next to my car. I don't mean to be rude, but I'm not chancing it. I'm not going to risk having someone steal my daughter.

October 31, 2000

Happy Halloween! This is the most screwed up holiday in the world. A day that encourages children to take candy from strangers. Strangers with fake blood and a noose around their necks.

Un-Perfect

I wonder what Parker was thinking as we made our way around fake headstones, said hello to passing witches, and rang the doorbell next to a body with a fake knife in its chest?

"That's okay honey, yes, it appears the owners of this home stabbed someone to death. Now let's beg for candy. Fingers crossed for Reese's cups!"

Parker doesn't have the capability of understanding the alphabet yet, but what she is hearing loud and clear is that it's okay to step over a dead body to beg for candy.

There are some good costumes out there. And what about the kids that don't say "Trick or Treat?" They just stare at me through their masks. I get the shivers wondering if it really is a costume or if they just finished someone off in the field with the kitchen knife and I'm next on their list.

But I wonder about all the holidays and what we're teaching our children. Parker is not old enough to understand yet, but next year, Santa is going to be a big hit around our house. I feel like I'm insulting her intelligence by explaining the concept of this phenomenon. An overweight man rides around the world with flying reindeer and squeezes his fat ass into everyone's fireplaces.

Normally, we would all be terrified of a stranger sneaking into our home in the middle of the night while we are sleeping, but this one is different. He leaves gifts instead of pulling out a 9mm and robbing our home of all its goodies.

If anything, I'm teaching my child that strangers are welcome in our home as long as he's in an ugly red suit and claims to fly. "Ding dong. Hi, I'm Santa. I see you have a fire going, so I need to come through the front door. So, where does Mommy keep all those credit cards?"

And how long am I supposed to lie to her? I was *twelve* when I learned there was no Santa. My friends were going to second base with boys and I was leaving notes for a mythical obese man in a flying sleigh. I think I had cigarettes on one of my lists. How could my parents not have known that I was too old to believe in that shit? At some point, "condoms and wine coolers" would have been on my list. How embarrassing.

Parker is still young. I haven't told her any lies yet. I'm still clean. I've screwed up almost everything else in her life, but this is still a clean slate. I don't want to ruin it by lying to her.

November 11, 2000

So Palm Beach County is going to MANUALLY recount 462,657 ballots. This Presidential election between Bush and Gore is more insane than having a newborn baby. I can't imagine if someone told me I had to be a part of that process. I'd be counting and recounting and recounting my little pile. And then I'd question if THAT was right, so I'd do it again. Years later I would worry that some sheets of paper stuck together and I did it wrong.

A little pile of ballots is going to determine who will run our country. And it will be done BY HAND. Why don't they just haul in the actual voters and corral them into little "playpens" of 1,000 and count their heads? That seems about as efficient and accurate as counting sheets of

Un-Perfect

paper.

11/12/00 Sunday Muffins At Mom's

My sisters and their families had stuff going on, so it was just me, Derek and Parker today. It's always special to have my parents all to myself. Being the baby of the family, I was born into sibling rivalry. Kari had four years to soak up my parents all alone. I can't imagine what that would be like. I feel lucky when I get two hours.

Mom said she would pay for my Lasik eye surgery for a Christmas present! My parents are giving me the gift of sight (and appearance). I'll be having it done in a couple of months. This is amazing. Thank you, thank you, thank you, thank you! I'm not even worried about what they could do to my eyes. Just do whatever needs to be done so I don't have to wear juice glasses strapped to my head anymore.

What would I do without my parents? Here's the problem: My parents are so great that I'm never going to live up to the standard they've set. This planet feels like a safer place just because they're in it and I don't think I'm doing the same for Parker. I think her world feels worse because of me.

I try explaining this concept to Mom and she says, "Oh Kelly, we've made plenty of mistakes. We're not perfect." I don't believe her. I still don't think my parents have made any mistakes. I've already made a billion. That can't be good enough.

December 10, 2000

I worry constantly about someone kidnapping Parker. There are weird people everywhere.

Last week a woman from daycare said someone tried to steal her son at Target. It was caught on videotape and everything. She said, "Kelly, I just turned my head to throw away a wrapper and I turned back and my son was GONE!"

This is horrifying. I have to be able to lean over and look at strawberries when I'm at the grocery store. I have throw things away too. I have to tie my shoe if the laces are un-tied. The point is, I can't stare at Parker 24/7.

Anyone can come up and steal her from me. All it takes is one second. One second when I take my eyes off her and she could be gone.

Un-Perfect

December 29, 2000

Parker is sitting, rolling over, and talking all the time. Colic feels like a distant memory. I wonder if the physical therapy worked its magic on the colic. I've heard of people bringing their babies to chiropractors to straighten out their necks and backs after being tucked into a belly for nine months. It makes sense, but it scared me to death thinking they could paralyze her. It just wasn't worth the risk.

Speaking of risks, she rolled off the bed the other day and Derek almost had a heart attack. You wouldn't think laying your baby on a bed while changing clothes is a risk, but it is. Risks are in the air around us and we can't avoid them. It drives me crazy because I can't see them or control them. Derek is convinced she has a concussion and is currently in the living room making her follow his finger back and forth over and over again.

I'm just glad the first accident didn't happen on my shift. I wouldn't be able to sleep knowing I took my eyes off her and let my guard down long enough to cause damage. She's grabbing everything and shoving stuff into her mouth like an addict. I'm jumping to her rescue constantly; I'm preventing her death at every given second. It's exhausting.

Not as tiring as colic, but a different kind of panic that wears me down. It's like I traded in colic for death defying panic. I simply graduated to a more intense anxiety. The colic wasn't life or death, but swallowing a Lego? That's survival. And she's not even crawling yet. I have no idea how I'll contain her when she's on the go. I want to wrap her in bubble wrap and duct tape her to my body. Would it be weird to walk around with her in the Baby Bjorn until she's eighteen?

I constantly check her crib for anything that could have fallen into it. You never know, a dime could fall into her crib and she'll stuff it in her mouth sometime during the night when I'm sleeping and I'll wake up and discover a tragedy from which I'll never recover. It's overwhelming to understand all the accidents that could happen. They lurk around every light socket, every step, every toy. Everything is dangerous.

I keep waiting for a reason to panic because that is all I have known since the day she was born. Now that it's quiet, I'm alone with my thoughts and I'm learning I don't have good ones.

In a weird way, I miss the distraction of all the screaming. I was too tired to worry, but now I'm aware of all the danger and uncertainty. When we remove noise, all we have is our thoughts. And my thoughts are noisy. I can't seem to focus on one calm thing because it always leads to, "What if?" What if she hits her head against a doorknob? What if she gets sick? What if she chokes on a toy?

It's impossible. I can't prevent every misfortune in the world. This is an overwhelming thought to me and lately, I've been swimming in it, finding it hard to breathe. I start cutting rows into the insides of my cheeks and soon feel the roadmap of pain and healing.

DEREK

12/30/01

Man, it feels good to sleep and get more of our life back. We're on easy street now that the colic is gone and Parker's sleeping through the night. Yes, I

Un-Perfect

thought Kelly was a barbaric bitch for making her cry it out, but it worked. I felt like I was neglecting and abusing my baby girl. If I'm honest, I'm still not comfortable with how it was done, but sleep is awesome.

Kelly still worries about EVERYTHING. I guess my thought is that if Parker swallows a Barbie shoe, she'll poop it out. Kelly immediately fast-forwards to the worst possible scenario. Why worry about shit that hasn't happened? It is a total and complete waste of time.

Yes, I pick up stuff to try and prevent it from happening, but I don't go to bed like she does, thinking about the safety of her crib and what if a button falls off her jammies. What a waste of time.

I don't get it. Seems exhausting to me, but whatever.

Note: I'm curious about when the sex life returns? I mean, now that we're over the colic, I'm wondering if sex will get back on track?

Oh but wait, has Kelly considered that we could fall off the bed while doing it? WHAT IF we break our necks because we fall off the bed while having sex? WHAT IF??!!!

That's a risk I'm willing to take. HA!

January 24, 2001

I finally feel like I'm coming back to me again. I figured I should do something for myself instead of sitting around worrying about all the things that could be detrimental to Parker's health and well being. So I started running.

More like I'm walking with a hop. In Sketchers.

Derek doesn't think I'll commit to running, so he doesn't think we should spend the $100 since money is tight. They're not even tennis shoes, they're mules. So they flop on my heels as I "run", which is a little annoying.

I see all the other people jogging and they look so refreshed and happy. How can I go wrong? I've already run a 5k. Sure, I almost died, but that was because I actually tried running the entire thing.

I had the Lasik eye surgery this week! What a miracle. The gift of sight is priceless. I can't believe I see 20/20 without glasses. Waking up to see the alarm clock is heavenly since I haven't been able to do that since the 80's.

I wore the eye protectors for three days longer than the doctor suggested. Today was the first day without them. As I was changing Parker's diaper, she reached up and poked me right in the eye. I have no idea if I'll go blind.

Un-Perfect

It's probably going to get infected because her finger was all spitty. She pulled it out of her mouth - a string of spit from her mouth to my eyeball - and poked me right in the eye. What if bacteria builds up where she touched it and then the cornea heals over it and then I'll need to have my eyeball totally removed? What if I get cancer in my eye? I rarely do anything for just me anymore and now it might be ruined.

February 17, 2001

She crawls everywhere. We were in a store and I set her down and she started crawling away from me. Anyone could have taken her from me.

What would I do if someone was bold enough to reach down and run away with her in their arms? I'm not a strong runner and I'm not big enough to tackle someone.

Everyone can see that I'm not a strong mother and wouldn't put up much of a fight. I'm skin, bones and smiles. No muscle. Anyone could clock me over the head and take my baby away from me. I feel like I have a target on my back.

February 24, 2001

I swear someone is always behind me, lurking, ready to strangle me. I keep looking over my shoulder, but no one is there. What is up with that? I'm always on guard in case someone tries to kill me and steal my sweet daughter.

March 12, 2001

Parker is crawling and pulling herself up and I'm standing on the sidelines chewing my fingernails off. There are dangerous things everywhere.

I was chopping an onion today for dinner and she almost reached the knife on the counter. I just left the knife on the counter thinking everything was fine. What if I wasn't watching and she grabbed the knife and fell on it? I want to keep her in the playpen, but she hates that thing.

The other day I was doing laundry and she leaned into the dryer because I left the door open. What if I didn't realize she fell into it and I turned it on? That could've killed her. I can't believe how reckless I am.

Derek picked up clothes from the dry cleaners on his way home from work today. He walked in carrying all those hangers and plastic; I almost had a heart attack. Looks like dead people hanging in plastic. Why am I the only one bothered by that image? I hate plastic bags. And he doesn't even knot them when he throws them away. Parker could dig into the trash and put a plastic bag over her head. It could

Un-Perfect

happen and he doesn't knot them. Drives me crazy.

Most people go to bed counting their blessings; I go to bed counting bypassed disasters.

She says, "Mama" and "Dada", but hasn't connected it to us. So when she says, "Mama" I look at her and say, "That's ME! I'm your Mama!" I'm her mama. I love being her mama.

Right now, I'm her everything and as she grows up, little by little, I'll need to step down from my pedestal. She'll need me less and less and the magnitude of my role will slowly transfer from me to her. She'll share big things with friends, lovers, and her own children some day.

But right now, I'm her everything and I'm honored. I hope I'm doing a good job. I know I'm a freak about keeping her safe, but that's just until she gets a little older.

4/26/01 Sunday Muffins At Mom's

It's my 31st birthday today! I love, love, love my birthday. I don't know how else to explain it other than I just wake up feeling extra special. Kari will leave a voicemail at work singing "Happy Birthday." Mom will call in the morning and if I'm not at my desk, will go into a diatribe about how she loves me so much and wishes me a great day. Kim will come through with the birthday call around lunch and we'll chat about any plans I

118

may have. Dad waits until the actual party at their house to give me a big squeeze and sing "Happy Birthday" off-key on purpose to be funny.

When it's someone's birthday, we replace Sunday Muffins with a birthday party. And I love it. Even though I'm thirty-one, I still make a wish and blow out the candles on Mom's special chocolate-chocolate cake, complete with ice cream on the side. This year I'm wishing for health and happiness for my family and me. In the very least, I'm wishing for my daughter to stay accident-free and continue living.

We'll take a family picture, me front and center with the cake and candles plopped right under my face. We do the automatic timer on the camera, so Dad will set it, then sprint across the kitchen and take his place next to Mom in the back of all the other smiling heads.

As the camera blinks the warning light that it will snap soon, Dad always proclaims something to make us laugh. So instead of the standard, "Say Cheese!" he'll say something like, "Okay…Everyone say, 'PACKERS SUCK!'" That one was special for Derek because he's not a Vikings fan.

Un-Perfect

Other birthday picture proclamations that replaced the traditional "Say Cheese!":

> STUPID!
>
> DENNIS IS AN IDIOT!
>
> NERD!
>
> PARKER IS A CRYBABY!
>
> KARI FARTED!

And he always shouts it from the back of the group, like a town crier from the 20's. We all wait to see what he'll say and it always makes us smile. People are laughing and piling on top of each other. Everyone is holding whatever little kid is too short to see over the top of the counter, faces smashed close together, and there will always be one making a stupid face or Kim will close her eyes on purpose and say, "What - I blinked!" And then we have to go through the entire debacle again and Dad will proclaim, "KIM'S A DORK!"

Everyone is there: Mom & Dad, sisters, brothers-in-law, nieces and nephews, and of course, Derek and Parker. We'll all gather 'round the kitchen counter, which is too small for our growing family, but we don't care. We'll reach across the counter, arms crossing over arms, to grab milk, a fork, a plate. I imagine all those criss-crossing arms looking like our own personal safety net.

Maybe it's the gathering of all my loved ones that makes it so awesome. It's the one time of the year where I'm allowed to be self-centered and bask in the fact that everyone made a special effort to be there for me. For one day out of the year, I allow the love in without worrying if it will go away. Well, at least I try.

May 13, 2001

While Derek was driving today, I kept watching the road below. God, that would hurt if I just opened the door and jumped out. I could have unlocked the door and jumped out while he was driving 60 mph.

I even put my hand on the door handle. I don't know why, I just did. I could have opened the door and jumped out onto the freeway.

It would hurt, wouldn't it? I wonder how bad it would hurt and how long I would feel it? But why would I even consider it? Why bother thinking about it? I don't want to do it.

Un-Perfect

May 19, 2001

Parker's first birthday! I can't believe she's one already. Last week was terrible trying to figure out what to buy, what to make, who to invite, where we will all sit. Too many decisions. I just want to enjoy it, but I can't because I get stuck on all the decisions.

How is she eating cake when I'm still looking for her bellybutton scab that fell off? So much of this year was a delirious blur, I can't even comprehend that we are celebrating her first birthday. Her hair is in ponytails for the first time today and I almost cried because she looks older. Thank goodness she still has the baby dimples on her knuckles and her ankles have that "baby fat wrinkle" where her pudgy legs meet her pudgy ankles. Evidence that she is still a baby. She is so beautiful. I love her more than anyone I've ever loved in my entire life.

And now her party is here and I'm worried she's going to have an allergic reaction to the cake. She's never had cake before, how do I know she's not allergic to it? And my sister just gave her whole milk without asking me if it's okay. She just assumes it's okay and it's not. What if Parker is allergic to milk? It makes me angry. Hello, I'm Parker's mother and need to monitor everything. Why doesn't my sister understand that?

Anyway, since Parker screamed her way through infancy, I feel robbed of the baby stage. I spent so many months panicking about how to fix her pain, I couldn't understand how to breathe in the experience and hold onto it while it was here. I still don't know how to do that. When will I learn how to do that?

She is totally content moving forward and I'm stuck wishing for the past that didn't happen. But she's happy being one. She's excited to be running around with her sippy cup saying, "juice!"

She's pulling me forward while I say, "Wait! Wait! Stop!" But there is no stopping. She only knows how to grow. That's the beautiful part of being a child. They don't wish for what was. They treasure what *is*. How can I get that back?

She's not traumatized by any of my panic. The other day I was changing the garbage and she walked up and grabbed the plastic bag. She grabbed it and tried walking away with it. I panicked and yelled "NO! DANGEROUS! BAD!" I know someone whose daughter suffocated in a plastic bag. It happened. I can't believe it almost happened to Parker too. She grabbed that plastic bag and if I wasn't looking, Parker could have put it over her head. I can't stand that thought, but I can't stop thinking about it.

I'm still stressed and panicked long after the reason for the stress and panic have been removed. The garbage bag incident happened hours ago, yet I'm still thinking about it. My fight or flight button is still activated and I don't know how to turn it off. How do I turn it off and just let it be? She didn't put that bag over her head. But she *could have* and that's what makes me crazy.

But scary thoughts aside, I look at her and can't believe I'm lucky

Un-Perfect

enough to have her be mine. Of all the children that could be born into this world, I think I got the best one.

LIFE CHAPTER 2:

CONFUSION

When a soul breaks, the sound is quiet.

The noise of fear, panic, worry, doubt, terror

Spin silently inside the core.

The only witness to the orbit of your soul

Is you.

What if you look inside

and what you see horrifies you?

Un-Perfect

"Confusion and Terror"

I had this picture taken to see if I looked normal.

The OCD hit hard that day, making me feel like a monster.

I was so confused about what was happening to me.

I was shocked to see that I looked normal. Happy even.

To this day, it's difficult to believe I smiled through

the terror, confusion and emotional pain.

May 21, 2001

Now that the colic is gone, everyone thinks I'm on easy street. That can't be further from the truth. The anxiety is not finished, I'm just moving it around - like pushing peas on my plate.

Sometimes I worry about my health, or about Parker's safety, or even whether Derek will leave me. Whatever the focus of my anxiety, I latch onto it and go full force, thinking about it constantly.

I'm finding things to worry about. If everything seems fine, I find something that could make it "not fine." Anything could happen. Anything.

Someone recently told me about a woman that tragically died. She had a headache, so her husband brought her into the hospital and she ended up stroking out and died. Right there. That's it. No chance for goodbyes, hugs or apologies.

To make the story more tragic, she had children and they're all devastated and asking when Mommy is coming back. How does her husband explain that she's not?

This is horrible and it can happen to me. All I can think about now is the headache I had last week. For God's sake, who hasn't had a headache? Is everyone just balancing on the cusp of life and death and all it takes is a common headache to tip us to the other side? That's terrifying.

Parker and Derek recovered from the colic and I'm sinking into a pool of anxiety and worthlessness. It doesn't make sense and it pisses me off. I want

Un-Perfect

to be colic-recovered and normal like them. I pretend to be happy all the time because that is what people expect but sometimes it's unbearable.

Here's the truth: As much as I loathed the screaming, I was grateful for a scapegoat. When I'm doing a crappy job at anything I like having a reservoir of excuses. When I golf, it's too windy. If I have a report due, the system is too slow. I don't like the playing field to be level, because then it's just me and everyone else. No handicap.

I'm never going to be perfect like everyone else and I'll never compare. Falling a little short is one thing, but failing miserably is a hearty insult to my expectations. I hate the idea of being insufficient at anything. I'm competitive to a fault. Everything is a competition to me.

Everyone thinks it's totally natural for me to empower the life of another human being. What if I screw her up and she's miserable her entire adult life because of me? I can't believe I'm forming her being, her thoughts, her perspective on the world, her attitude, her gratitude, everything. The expectations are suffocating me.

What if I have a particularly awful day and I teach her to be an ungrateful bitch? What if I can't reverse the effects of a crappy day? Am I not allowed to have a bad day for fear that I'm teaching my child to be ungrateful?

Parker and Derek hardly exist to me because I'm so caught up in myself, wondering how I appear to the outside world. Do I look like I know what I'm doing? Am I faking it well enough to trick everyone into thinking I'm a good mother?

I'm certainly not fooling myself. If my body could display the worry my head feels, it would be a tornado. I'm spinning with questions and concerns. There is a saying, "Fake it 'till you feel it". That is how I'm living right now. I am hoping no one sees through my phony veneer.

Derek kisses me goodbye in the morning knowing that everything is fine. He thinks I'm a champ, so I'm apparently fooling him. Why does he trust me? I could drop the hot iron on her while ironing my clothes or she could grab something and choke on it when I'm in the shower.

I don't trust me, so why does he? Doesn't he understand that I have no veto power against the unknown (and uncontrollable) situations?

I worry about everything and people blow it off and say, "Every mother is a worrywart." But my God, do they worry to the extent I do? Do they worry they're a bad mother? Do they worry about all the crazy shit that could happen and kill people?

I'm taking "worrywart" to a new level. Instead of sleeping, I'm doing instant replays of the day over and over again in my head like ticker tape across the bottom of my brain: Did I look like a good mom today at the grocery store? Did I say something offensive to my neighbor? Why did I reprimand Parker for getting out of her bed? Did my thong ride up and out of my jeans today at work? Did I tie a knot in the plastic bag before I threw it away? It just goes and on and on. My energy is bankrupt.

May 23, 2001

"You can do anything!"

This is meant to be a positive statement, but I hear it like this: Yes, I can do anything. I can jump out of the car when Derek is driving, I can veer off the bridge and break through the cement barrier, I can die of cancer, I can slice my wrists, I can scream in Target, I can forget to tie a knot in a plastic bag and Parker could grab it out of the

Un-Perfect

trash and suffocate, I can have a nervous breakdown.

I can do anything and it scares me to death.

May 24, 2001

I feel like a shell, mimicking authentic life. A copycat. I pick and choose pieces of behavior that I admire and I copy them. I'm a chameleon of the masses so no one thinks I'm different. But it's exhausting always trying to be someone else.

Somewhere during my walk into motherhood, I lost **me.** *But where did I go? I've lost keys, money and shoes. But my own SELF?*

Isn't that supposed to be tucked inside my body for safekeeping? How did I lose that?

Lately, if someone cracks a joke I hesitate: "Would I have laughed at that before? I don't remember." I feel like people are expecting more of a show, but I don't remember what props I used. Was I pulling monkeys out of hats before? I know I was a fan of verbal tap dancing for everyone's entertainment, but I can't pull it off anymore.

It's like being thrown onto a movie set with no script - or even any idea what my character is supposed to be. I want to yell, "CUT!" It's embarrassing to keep blowing my lines and missing my cues.

I've never been socially inept, but now I feel confused and lost in conversation because I don't understand what an appropriate reaction would be. Sometimes I feel like I'm out of my body, watching someone else use it to talk, joke, laugh and listen. The other day my neighbor was talking about her divorce. "… and the child support he's offering is ridiculous, it won't even cover groce… *Am I really standing here right now? Maybe I'm really dead and I'm just watching another person having this conversation. Maybe my heart pounded so hard it just kicked me out of my body. I couldn't catch my breath a few seconds ago, so I must have died – because now I'm floating. Any minute now I'll realize this isn't real.*"

I've never felt like this before - I've always been social. It's in the core of who I am. When I was five-years-old I walked across the street and sat on a bucket while singing, "The Most Beautiful Girl In The World" to my neighbor Norm while he worked on his car. It's just who I am. Or who I used to be.

I love people. Well, I USED to love people. Conversation is like music and I've always understood the song. But now I can't even hear the basic beat of the drum. I'm staggering and stumbling trying to appear charismatic and true.

DEREK

5/27/01

I can't believe Parker is one. A year ago she couldn't lift her head and now she's running around and laughing. Kel's getting rest and cracking jokes again. I lost her for a while there, when we were both tired, but she's back and I have my wife again.

We're a married couple with a baby. That is still so weird to me.

Un-Perfect

I remember when Kelly told me she was pregnant. I honestly never thought it would happen, so I never really thought about being someone's dad. Girls do that. They think about who they'll date, marry, and think about being a mom. Guys don't. At least I didn't. Each day was just a day. I didn't think that far ahead about my life. I still don't.

I'm just a shy guy that happened to get a girl to marry him. And now we have a kid. And a house. Sometimes I think, "Holy shit, this really is my life." It's kind of this weird thing that happens because I move one day at a time. So one day I'm not married and one day I am. One day I'm not a dad and one day I am.

It's almost like I don't notice things moving in a direction until after it's done. Like now. Today I'm thinking, "I really am a married man with a kid. I'm a DAD, man." Crazy.

Note: Parker's new thing is sitting in the fridge. IN it. The door is left wide open, letting all the cool air out, but I don't care. I let her do it.

May 25, 2001

I had a nightmare. Or was it real? I dreamed that I killed someone and I was driving around trying to figure out how to quietly dispose of the body. She was in the trunk of my car, a woman, I remember that now, and I didn't know why I killed her.

I desperately wanted to turn back time, but it was too late. I already killed her and her blood was in the trunk of my car and everyone was going to find out. My family was going to be shocked and disappointed, so I was going to dig a hole for the body, then run away to Mexico so no one could find me.

But I knew I'd never escape. I woke up crying. I didn't want to go to jail because my daughter would be embarrassed to have me for a mother.

Rationally, I knew it was a dream, but I still checked my trunk to ease my worry. And if it was a dream, why do I feel so guilty and sad?

I'm so sorry for even dreaming it.

I'm so sorry.

May 28, 2001

I have no reason to be anything other than a perfect mother and wife. I have a husband that loves and supports me. I have a beautiful, healthy daughter. But I'm not perfect and the only blame for my discontent lies on my shoulders. If

Un-Perfect

I'm not happy, it is no one's fault but my own.

Everything is perfectly lined up for me, the road is paved with gold, yet I'm scared I'll get cancer or Parker will run into the street and get hit by a car. My world is so perfect that I no longer fit in it.

I don't feel comfortable with perfect because then my flaws are that much more apparent. I like things messy so I can make mistakes and no one will notice. But when things are perfect, everyone knows when something gets messed up.

There's a saying that if you can't spot the fuck- up in the group, it's you. Derek and Parker are happy and wonderful. I'm the fuck-up sitting in the corner biting her nails off, worrying about every bad possible outcome.

What is wrong with me?!?

I'm like a queen that won't leave her room to enjoy all her luxuries. I have good things in my life, but I am too preoccupied with worry, so it's impossible to enjoy it. And I know I need to turn off the switch and just enjoy it. But there is no switch. If there was an "OFF" button, I would have hit it already.

It would be so much easier to just be bad instead of always worrying if I'm doing the right thing. There would be no expectations, disappointment, or failure. I wouldn't be anxious about what anyone thought about me. It's exhausting to constantly analyze my behavior and worry if people are criticizing me. I replay my entire day when I go to sleep to calculate if I did the right things, what I could do better, and if there should be any apologies to anyone for my behavior.

I don't feel natural, so I need to appraise every situation. Joke equals laughter. I feel rough around the edges, sharp and to the point, computing my responses. Everyone around me is soft and open and easy. I want to be anyone but me.

I watch them with fascination now, acknowledging that I was one of them once. When did I become separated from the whole? I've been walking down a road with my head down, lost in thought, staring at my feet for the past year and now that I look up, I don't recognize where I am. It's that feeling of being lost in the store when you're with your mother. You're not lost necessarily. You know she's there somewhere, but you're scared and lonely even though you are surrounded by people.

I watch everyone, wishing it were that easy for me. The slight touch of an arm while they laugh or leaning their heads together while a secret is shared. I'm missing that ease of communication and I don't know where to find it. I've had it all my life, that extrovert gene that allowed me to float into a room of strangers and leave with five new friends. I could travel the world without an itinerary and make a friend in every country.

Now I can't even befriend myself. I don't know who I am, who I'm supposed to be, or who I was. I keep rewinding the tape, thinking back to how I would have acted before I had Parker, like researching old movies playing in my head. I don't recognize the woman in the movies, but I know it was me.

If I have a date with Derek, I think back to a date we had before Parker and I try to copy it. We went to a movie, I held his hand, we laughed. What did we talk about? Now all we talk about is Parker, which is great, but when we try talking about something else our smiles fade with a deep breath and it's silent. Sparks fall in the air like dying fireworks.

I can't replicate my old self and it's frustrating. Everything feels

Un-Perfect

tentative and embarrassing while I try to grasp at my old behavior. We look around the restaurant, uncomfortable and awkward, sensing the missing third person that was left home with a sitter.

We're trying to scratch under the surface to see if there is any of the old stuff left behind, but we're not finding anything, so now we have to start building the foundation again. What a shame that all the work we've done is not in my memory bank anymore. Why can't I remember what we were like before?

June 1, 2001

I was on the bus this morning and I looked at a woman seated across from me. I was looking at her red heels, worn-out camel colored leather briefcase and her beautiful blonde wavy hair. I wished I was her – I bet she has a great life. She was listening to music and swaying her head to the beat, unaware that I was watching her.

Out of the blue, I wondered if she would beg for mercy or fight back if a stranger walked up and tried to kill her. Wait, what? Why on earth did I think a thought like that? That's terrible, I didn't want to think about that. What kind of person thinks like that?

I looked out the bus window and started biting the insides of my cheeks until I felt them bleed. Over and over again, pinching that soft flesh between my teeth. I needed to be in control of something, even if it was self-inflicted pain. I tried cutting a perfect row on each side, but one cut was too low and the line wasn't perfect. All day I felt that inconsistency and it aggravated me.

I know fear. It's been my friend for most of my life. When I was in seventh grade I had my very own stalker that threatened to kill my family if I tattled on her. Every single godforsaken day she would walk by my class and flash a knife she carried around in her shoe.

Maybe the fact that I was 75 lbs, wore glasses, and a headgear put a nice big target on my ass. I was easy to push around and I'm sure my stalker could sense it like a predator smelling its prey. I was too terrified to even cry. Instead, I would get numb and pull out of my body and watch it all happen from somewhere outside of me. I would sit there like stone, thinking maybe I died and just left the shell.

Sometimes fear can instigate the fight-or-flight systems. I think I lost the "fight" piece of the puzzle long before seventh grade. Everyone has a fight-or-flight reaction to survival, but I simply own flight-or-flight. Fear drives me away from threat, never toward it. I'm a coward.

My stalker situation ended on the very last day of school when she requested that I meet her by the skating rink after school. I was exhausted and relieved in a sick way that she was finally going to kick the shit out of me. Everyone was gathered for the big fight, but she walked right by me without a punch.

As frightened as I was of my seventh grade stalker, it doesn't compare to being afraid of myself. What I experienced on the bus this morning is making me scared of *me*.

It's this weird fear seeping into the inside of my body and coiling around my head. How do I fight a bully inside of my own mind?

Un-Perfect

June 2, 2001

I'm in constant survival mode even though I have nothing to survive. I can't sleep because nightmares are always waiting for me.

Every night I wait for the waves of terror to lap up and take me under its current. My worst fears swell up and take me into its suffocating fold. I "live" out my worst tragedies while I sleep. Someone stole Parker, her head went through one of the slats in the crib, she was in a plastic bag fighting for her life...

It's like my own personal hell that I'm forced to visit when I fall asleep every night. I wake up sweating and paralyzed with fear. I don't move, I don't breathe.

I blink and think.

What is this? Is something going to happen to her and these nightmares are my warning? I can't get peace even when I sleep. I start biting the insides of my cheeks. They're all bumpy and scarred up now, rows of inflicted pain that I've created on my own body.

I bite and pinch the flesh with my teeth until I can taste the blood. No matter, it always heals. I need to feel something in me heal.

June 3, 2001

Another nightmare. I killed someone. A man. He was huge and powerful, but he was threatening to kill me, so I attacked him first. I used the edge of a sheet of paper to cut his throat and I had to do it over and over and over again. Slowly slicing an open wound.

All I could think about was how painful it must have been for this man while I kept cutting him. I couldn't stand to see all the blood and I really couldn't stand that I was killing him. I felt so bad.

I ran away while someone else finished him off with the paper. Even though I know it's a dream, I still feel terrible, like I really did it. So guilty and panicked.

June 5, 2001

Why can't anyone see that I'm not who I used to be? I'm so disappointed that people who claim to love me can't see that I'm not the same and I need help. Can't they see this seething monster underneath my skin?

My nightmares and "daymares" are not something normal people do. Why do they keep saying that I'm normal and everything is fine when I tell them that I worry about things?

Un-Perfect

I try telling them about seeing things happening to Parker. For example, I can see her walking down the driveway and see a car coming down the road and hitting her. I can see her little body being pelted by the grill and I can hear the brakes of the car. Then I imagine how the driver will get out of the car, panicking, and someone will need to call 911 while I hold my dying baby in my arms in the middle of the street. I can't stand it, it's awful.

No one seems to think this is disturbing, but me. They say, "Oh I know, it's scary to think about all the things that could happen to our kids, but you can't spend your time worrying about it." I'm not CHOOSING to spend time worrying about it. That's the thing. These thoughts come into my head without an invitation.

When I'm at work I'll say, "Okay, I'll pull a report that will show [flash of my dad hanging from a noose] all of the orders year-to-date. That way we can forecast the budget appropriately." I'm streaming a conversation while horrific images inject themselves into my head, interrupting my life. I wish they would at least leave me alone during the day and save up for the nightmares instead.

And to be fair, I'm not telling anyone this part of it. I'm hiding the whole story, keeping it a secret. I'm seeing shit without my consent and there is no association to what I'm doing or discussing. Budgets and hanging from a noose don't live together in any world. That's like a store offering body piercing and miniature golf. It just doesn't make sense.

I have no control over my thinking and these daymares are beginning to freak me out. Maybe if I get some sleep they'll go away. Maybe they are just a

140

symptom of exhaustion. But I can't sleep. My nightmares wake me up and I spend the rest of the night with electric anxiety running through my veins, pumping my heart too fast for my breath.

6/7/01 Sunday Muffins at Mom's

I sit at the counter and my family asks normal questions as if I'm normal. Apparently, I don't look like a monster on the outside.

No one sees it. My sisters ask about work and Mom asks about my weekend as if I'm perfectly fine. I feel like we're playing a game. "If I answer their questions as if I'm normal, then we can all pretend that I'm normal." But can't they see I'm not the same person? Or am I faking it that well? Or did I just tell them that I'm really tired?

I think I made an excuse for my anti-social behavior. Oh that's right, I did. I told them I was up all night with an allergy attack.

Which technically, is not a lie. It was the anxiety attack that kept me awake, which led to an allergy attack. I woke up to hear a train coming through around two in the morning and then the anxiety seeped right in

Un-Perfect

my bones. It doesn't even give me a 5-minute warning. It just sets in as soon as I start to wake up. My heart pounds so hard I can see my chest moving, then I start sweating, and then I start worrying about the day and play it out in my head.

So really, I've already been to Muffins and worried that I don't appear normal to everyone. I was here at 2:00 a.m., sitting at this counter, pretending to be normal for everyone's benefit. It's exhausting doing things twice: Once during my morning anxiety attack and again when it happens in real life.

Anyway, I feel like they're talking about me when I leave. As soon as I shut the front door, I bet they all start in with, "Did she seem totally out of it to you? She seemed wacky today. Do you think there's something wrong with her?"

I expect they'll all ridicule me behind my back, which is much deserved, because I *am* wacky. I just wish they'd come out and say it to my face instead of talking behind my back. At least then it won't be a secret anymore.

June 8, 2001

Parker woke up in the middle of the night last night. I hate it when she does this because it requires me to get up without having time to get my guard up. I never know if I'm going to be bombarded with weird thoughts or not.

Last night as I was stroking her forehead and singing, "You Are My Sunshine" I thought, "What if I accidentally put a pillow over her face?" Somewhere on this planet, that has happened. A mother has done that to her daughter. I can't believe it. I can't believe a mother could be capable of such harm to her own child. How could anyone harm her own child? I can't stand that thought. What kind of world do we live in? It's so dangerous. A child can't even trust her own mother.

I don't want to harm Parker in any way. I'm her mother and my job is to protect her. Even if it's from my own thoughts. I hate thinking of every single possible way that she could be harmed. It's endless.

What kind of mother thinks these thoughts? I finished the song and then crawled back into bed. Then the worrying began. I wasn't sure if I did anything to her, so I went back in to check her breathing. Yes, she was breathing, so I went back to bed.

Then I got up again to make sure I didn't do anything *that* time. Thank

Un-Perfect

God, she was breathing. After doing this about seven or eight times, I woke Derek up to check on her to make sure she's fine. He crawled back in and I said, "She's okay?" "Yeah", he sighed. "Now go to sleep." Thank God he's here with me. Thank God, thank God, thank God.

I would have liked to sleep, but I had an anxiety attack instead. I couldn't breathe and started sweating. I tried calming myself down. "She's fine, she's healthy, and alive. He just checked on her. You didn't do anything wrong." It didn't work.

I started cutting into the sides of my cheeks while I tried convincing myself that I'm a good person. I hate the thoughts that just pop in and pop out. It's like a sadistic magic show that begins and ends without me buying a ticket. And then it goes away as if nothing ever happened.

Sometimes I'm left wondering if I really did just think those thoughts an hour ago or did I just make it up? I feel crazy, wondering why I'm being forced to think up this stuff. It doesn't make sense.

What the hell IS THIS???

June 9, 2001

I just know that someone is tracking me down and wanting to kill me. I can't explain it, but I feel like someone is always behind me ready to strangle me.

Sometimes it's even hard to breathe. I keep looking over my shoulder, but no one is there. I bet they're waiting until my guard is down and I will be too tired to fight back. I know this is a strategy to get rid of me so he/she can take

Parker away from me and sell her in another country.

I can't sit next to the passenger side door in the car anymore. I sit sideways facing Derek so I don't stare at the road whizzing by below me. I always wonder what it would be like to jump when we're on the freeway. The car behind us would be shocked to see a body fall out of our car and they would run me over and it would hurt so badly. I would be in so much pain, but then it would be over. The pain would be over.

June 10, 2001

What if I sleepwalk and do something bad?

I sleepwalk a lot. All of a sudden, I'll wake up just as I'm crawling back into bed and wonder, "Where was I just now? What did I just do?"

Then I worry I suffocated Parker or Derek, so I'll have to get back up and check to make sure she's breathing. Then I check to make sure he's breathing.

But then as I crawl back into bed again, I think maybe I checked her breathing, and then suffocated her. Because I remember checking her breathing, but I don't remember if I did anything bad after that. So I'll go back in there, check her breathing, then come back to bed and think I

Un-Perfect

killed her…on and on and on.

I'll do this for about an hour and then finally wake Derek and ask him to check her. When he comes back and says she breathing, I can go to sleep. I trust him. I don't trust myself. I can't be the last one in her room, because I don't trust that I left her safe and sound. Why is that? I love her with all my heart so why would I think I would harm her in any way?

"You were just in there thirty seconds ago" he'll say. "Why do I have to go in there?" It is more of a gripe than a question. If he truly asked why, I'm not sure how I would answer the question. Being truthful would scare the shit out of him and he'd ask that I move out and live with my parents until I get my head straight.

I can see how it would all play out: He would be raking his hand through his hair like he always does when he's baffled and finally staring at me like he always does when he makes a solid decision. He'd shake his head back and forth and say, "This is fucking unbelievable, Kelly. You're not the woman I married. What do you want me to do? I have to protect our daughter. I love you, but I can't do this." Then he would leave me and I would never see Parker again.

I've played it out a million times in my head. It's already happened in my mind. Life just has to catch up with it. It's like TV being delayed a few seconds because the satellite signal has to return it to earth.

Real life is just a delayed form of our thoughts, isn't it? Each thought is like sending a rope to the stars and reeling it in. Fishing for life. With the thoughts I'm having lately, what exactly am I fishing for in life?

Maybe I'm just tired.

Yeah, I think it's just a sleep deprivation thing and I'll be fine once I start sleeping through the night. It's better than admitting I can't handle a perfect life. That is insane to me. Who can't tolerate a beautiful husband and daughter, a great job, house in the 'burbs, and a new car?

How can that be too much for anyone? If I can't live normally in this perfect life, then how could he trust that I would handle bigger things as we live out the rest of our marriage together? When he's eighty-five years old and needs a hip replaced, how can he trust that I'll take care of him? My God, what if something really *does* happen to Parker?

If I tell him about my daymares and nightmares, he will never depend on me again for anything. I'm the rock. I'm the one everyone depends on. I can't fail.

June 18, 2001

This morning on the bus I panicked because I forgot to check the front of my car for blood. I don't check it every day, but this morning for some reason, it seemed important for me to check and I didn't. What if while I was sleeping I got into my car and ran someone over? I sleepwalk almost every night and it scares me because I don't know what I'm capable of when my guard is down.

All day I police these horrific thoughts of death, my daymares - but what happens when my awareness is paused? What is to prevent me from acting out on these thoughts if I'm sleeping? I'm so vulnerable and not able to rationalize anything.

I didn't check the trunk either. What if I killed

Un-Perfect

someone and put him/her in the trunk? So all day at work, while I tried to figure out my client's budgets, I wondered if there was a body in the trunk of my car.

I talked with my friends about good sales on shoes, but conversations were interrupted constantly.

"Oh my God! Did you see Neiman Marcus has almost all their summer shoes at 40% off? Let's head [what if I open the trunk of my car and there is a dead body in there? What will I do?] over there at noon!"

I envy everyone else. They worry about normal things like bills, getting good deals on shoes, and fighting with their husbands about housework. They don't question the core of their being, wondering if they're good or bad. They get to go along their lives blissfully unaware that things could be so much worse than bouncing a check. I'm worrying if I killed someone in my sleep and I'll go to prison for the rest of my life. I'd give anything to worry about my bank account.

Everything is relative. Remember when your worst experience was not being asked to the prom? Or when you were finally asked to the prom, you couldn't find a dress that made your boobs appear bigger than they were? That was my biggest problem in the 80's. My lack of boobies. What a simple, beautiful time. My worries were so tiny they could fit on the tip of a finger.

How do we know which worries are actually rational and life-changing? Can we understand when our lives are starting to shift or do we suddenly find ourselves in the middle of it, wondering how we got there?

With each tick of the clock, the path we made in the snow fills with snowflakes. Each flake is so small you can't see any change... but when enough of them land, it fills in your footprint completely. You can't be sure you even took that step. All you know is that you're in an unfamiliar place and have no idea how to get back.

We lose ourselves during change. Not able to go back, but afraid to move forward, we sit in our own personal purgatory, until we have the guts to take another step.

I don't like where I'm going, but I can't seem to stop taking the steps forward to this place, wherever it is. I feel pulled, compelled to find this new place, even though it asks me to leave my old self at the door. My old footprints are covered with snow – I have no idea how I would ever get back to who I was before. Everything I used to be is lost and I'm left with this cheap imitation of the old me.

Where I'm standing now is scary. I don't even like haunted houses, but I can't get off this ride. It's already begun and I've paid the price with my soul. It keeps twisting and turning, craning its neck to see more gore, not getting enough of these terrifying thoughts.

I want to worry about trivial things like dishes in the sink again.

DEREK

6/18/01

Man, we are on easy street. We've got this parenting gig down now. We've been to hell and back with the colic and now it's time to sit back and have a beer.

I wired the deck with outdoor speakers last

Un-Perfect

weekend so Kel and I can hang out there after work and listen to Dave Matthews while Parker plays with her plastic grocery cart. She walks like Frankenstein. It's like her feet are made of cement blocks. It's funny.

But this sleepwalking/nightmare thing...the other night Kelly was screaming, "You have to protect us! He's in here!" I had to grab her wrists yelling, "KELLY! KELLY!" Trying to wake her up. Her hair was wet with sweat and she was shaking. Hell, I was shaking.

I had to search the entire house at 2:45 a.m. to make sure it was safe. My job as a husband and father is to keep my girls safe, but what am I supposed to do when the intruder is in a nightmare? How can I protect my family against that?

I don't even dream, so I really don't understand how bad nightmares can be. From the look on Kelly's face, it's pretty bad.

Kelly has me on "sleepwalking watch" which means that if she sleepwalks I'm supposed to wake her. Question: How the hell am I supposed to know if she's sleepwalking?

I hugged her and told her that I'll keep watch if she gets up through the night, but I don't see the big deal. She's a worrywart and likes to get up to feel

Parker breathing. Big deal.

Note: There's no way I'm going to wake up every single time Kelly gets up to check on Parker. I sleep like a rock.   I told her that line of bullshit to make her feel better. It's the best I can do. There's no way I'll wake up through the night to check on my wife. My alarm barely wakes me up.

June 20, 2001

What is a split personality and can a person "catch" it? I know it sounds crazy, but I feel like I'm two separate people.

On one hand, I'm nice and caring. My heart reaches out and wraps around the people I love. I help friends move, I bring soup to loved ones when they're sick, I hug, kiss and tickle Parker, and make buddies laugh at happy hour.

On countless occasions, people tell me I'm the happiest person they know; they want to know my secret. I don't have one. I simply try to distract myself with laughter to avoid being alone with my thoughts.

I feel like I'm pretending to be nice so I can control and manipulate people. I'm afraid I'm actually rotten to the core and fooling everyone into believing that I'm happy.

Un-Perfect

Which one is the "real" Kelly?

What if all these terrible thoughts are products of the real me? And the "fake me" is the nice one. What is happening to me??? I play this game with Derek all the time: What are you thinking right NOW!? He always plays along. "Uh well, actually I was thinking how cool it would be if I was Brett Favre. That would be sweet, wouldn't it? To be a professio…"

Then I tune out. No matter often I try and catch him off-guard, he's never thinking bad thoughts. Never. Sometimes he says he's not thinking at all. I can't believe it. "NOTHING? You didn't even have a single thought in your head at all?" He just shrugs and says, "Nope. Just sittin' here."

That is unbelievable to me. Not one thought was in his head. Is he stupid or Zen? I can't figure it out.

I was eating lunch with my friends at work recently. CNN had some breaking news about a homicide and I looked closely to make sure it wasn't me on the screen, catching footage of something horrible my split did while the normal side of me slept.

This is not a far-reached concept for me. I'm convinced I have a split personality. How else can I explain these little injections of horror into my normal life?

June 21, 2001

Andrea Yates killed her children. I don't know if it was a religious thing or if she was crazy. Everyone is talking about how she should get the death penalty and be locked up for life.   People are convinced that Andrea's children should have been taken from her and she didn't deserve to be a mother.

More times than I can count, my friends have said, "This woman makes me sick to my stomach." Me too.   I can't stand to even read about it.

This is why I'm not telling anyone the full story. Parker will be taken away from me.   Derek will leave me and I'll never see my daughter again.   Not that I don't deserve it, I do, but not yet.

This is what I worry about. I'll need to go away before Parker gets too old. Before I screw her up. Right now, she seems happy and smart. She loves life, so I haven't affected her too much yet. But I know I need to go away before I cause too much damage to her.

She'll have a better life without me. I'd rather have her remember me laughing, than being crazy. I'd rather go out on top while things are still relatively normal.

Besides, Derek is such an amazing father and I'm such a crappy mom. And Parker's such a pure, sacred, beautiful, loving, human being. People come into this world in such an incredible state of being. It's overwhelming to realize how much damage I can do. She was born perfect. And then there's me - screwing everything up. All that "perfect-ness" is getting ruined.

I don't do well with failure, and failing at motherhood is COLOSSAL . Why didn't I fail patrols in 5th grade or fail out of college? Why did motherhood have to be my failure? That's huge. I want to be like everyone else and fail at

Un-Perfect

stuff that doesn't matter. People suck at a lot of things, but not parenthood.

This epiphany sucks.

If could take back all my success and trade it for success in motherhood, I wouldn't hesitate to make a trade. Forget the Dean's List in college. Forget my job in advertising. Those things don't matter.

I'd trade it all for understanding how to be a good mother.

June 23, 2001

Why does everyone have it better than me? They all have these happy, shiny lives and every day is a struggle for me. It's not that I want their actual lives, but I want their confidence, peace and joy.

How do I get that? They're totally at ease with everything and I'm not. That would make me at "dis-ease". I have a disease then, so what is it? "Un-Joy"? Is that what I suffer from? "Un-Perfect"? Is that my disease?

My theory is this: Anything that interrupts the ease of life is disease. I don't give a shit if a medical book doesn't have what I'm experiencing in there. I have something that is disrupting my ease of life. It's breaking down my life, but what is it? What is banging down the door of my head and injecting gory, painful, visions and thoughts?

What is causing my "dis-ease"?

Kelly Nordstrom

Andrea Yates is all over the news with a term called postpartum psychosis. That could be my disease, but if I mention this to anyone, I'll be tossed in a psych ward and never see my family again. I keep thinking about the excruciating details of the Yates situation – I'm rolling it around in my head as if I was there witnessing the entire thing. I can't stand it. And it just keeps replaying over and over again. My brain doesn't want to turn it off. I want it to shut off, but it won't.

I keep playing the game with Derek. Yesterday I bombarded him. "What are you thinking NOW! Right NOW! What's in your head? Quick!" He just smiled, tossed his arm around my shoulder and said, "I was thinking you have a nice ass." That's it. That's his thought. I would cringe if he asked me what I was thinking about. What would I say? "Uh, I was thinking about how people die in plane crashes. Like, what are they thinking as the plane goes down and at what point do they just die of sheer terror and do body parts rain down from the sky after a plane explodes?" Thank God he never plays that game with me.

I honestly have nothing to do with these thoughts other than housing them in my head. They're like illegal squatters, hanging out in my psyche without paying rent. They come and go like drug dealers, smuggling in horrible thoughts. That's the drug I'm addicted to. Shitty thoughts.

It makes me so sad to think that people would hate me if they knew the real me. I don't want people to hate me. I want people to like me. All of me. But that's not reality. They would hate me if they really knew me. God, that makes me sad.

DEREK

6/24/01

What am I thinking RIGHT NOW?

I'm thinkin' I'd like to get laid.

6/25/01 Sunday Muffins at Mom's

As I sat at the counter, I looked around and realized that I don't belong in this family. If you looked at our family picture, you'd see the one that doesn't belong because she's not beautiful like the rest of them. Me.

I have curly hair, my sisters don't. They were homecoming candidates, I'm a nerd. Plus, they're totally confident in who they are – they are good to the core. I'm not a good person. We don't match.

I'm always stuck in a "too perfect" place where my faults and flaws stick out like sharp sticks. It's obvious that I'm adopted. They probably took me in to save me from the devil. I can see Mom saying, "Oh Ron, look at this poor thing. She's so sweet, we can't have her knowing she's the daughter of Satan." For some reason, they took me in as their own. I don't understand why; it's actually quite a sacrifice for them. They had such an amazing family without me.

My sisters both tried convincing me that I was adopted when I was little and I'd run to Mom, crying. "Is it TRUE?" She would wrap me in her arms and say, "Of course not. KARI! KIM! Knock it off – it's not funny!" I wonder now if they had family meetings after I went to bed to explain to Kari and Kim that my cover can't be blown. After all, they are doing their best to keep me safe and hidden from my real parents, who are probably truly psychotic demons that roam around killing people.

Derek doesn't know my secret. If he did, he would've never married me. He's just caught up in this. An innocent bystander while evil slips into bed with him every night. I feel bad for him. If I knew this earlier, I would not have sucked him into this horrible life with me.

So will my parents ever tell me about my *real* parents? Are they trying to find me? Do they want to hunt me down and slaughter me? Maybe that's who is following me. I should probably know what plans have worked in the past, so I can keep up the ruse, but I think it would ruin our family to reveal the secret. Once we start speaking openly about it, we'll all be danger. My real parents will want to kill all of us and I

Un-Perfect

can't have that. This family has been good to me. I'm fiercely protective of them.

In a way though, this is a relief. I understand now why I feel like a vicious person. And it's the perfect disguise because I'm such a nice person from a great family. I'm good by association because of my amazingly happy, perfect family.

No one would believe the revolting thoughts that gallop across my brain.

June 26, 2001

Someone is going to attack me and take my daughter.

I can feel him behind me, waiting and strategizing for the perfect time. It's that man that took our picture almost a year ago. I know that now. He probably looks at that picture every day and takes notes about our routine. He sees how exhausted I am and knows that he will have an easy time killing me. I keep looking behind me, but he's never there. He's sneaky.

Maybe it's my real father, the serial killer, keeping tabs on his daughter and granddaughter. I will beg and plead for him to kill me instead of Parker.

Please God, just let Parker live and be untouched by all this evil.

June 27, 2001

Why can't I just fit myself into the mold I had pictured for myself? I can write it down: Independent, happy, calm, confident. I want to be a paper doll so I can fold the paper tabs over my body and wear my happiness or confidence.

I know what I want, so why can't I just be it?

But I can't. This is not working and I can't tell anyone. If I did, they'll try helping me and I hate people helping me or coming to my rescue. It makes me feel inferior. Allowing someone to help me is like admitting defeat and weakness. It's giving another person permission to be superior to me. If someone is stronger than me, my ego will be pinned to the floor. I'll be defeated. Conquered.

In my job, I'd rather work all night than admit I had difficulty learning something. Then I would show up for an 8:00 a.m. meeting pretending that I finished it in an hour and got all kinds of rest. That's me, the big faker. I fake confidence, esteem, intelligence and worth. This is why people think I'm a good mom. I fake it.

Nothing is real. I feel like I'm living out a Broadway show pretending to be a character I studied. Most people would get home after a long day on the

Un-Perfect

stage, kick off their shoes and say, "Oh, thank God I can just be me." I don't know who I am, so I stay in character. Always.

The role I'm playing is complete with plastic smiles and laughter. It's not real. I'm on stage and everyone I love is milling about in the lobby having a great time while I study my lines and make sure I know my parts. They can see me from the audience, but I'm untouchable.

I don't want anyone to know what I'm dealing with, so I try extra hard to appear normal like everyone else.

June 27, 2001 3:34 a.m.

I'm tempted to sneak downstairs to see if the gas in my car is at the same level as it was when I parked it in the garage. How else will I know if my dreams are real or not?

Tonight I dreamed that I killed someone and I was in a frenzy trying to bury a body. I was so afraid of going to prison for the rest of my life and never seeing Derek and Parker again.

I woke up wheezing and gasping for air. The panic attack already started while I was dreaming. I was THAT CLOSE to dying - I don't think I was breathing, which why I woke up.

I started biting my cheeks to focus and remain calm.

Did I go anywhere while I was sleeping? When the sun comes up I will have to check the front of my car for

blood. I want to go down there now, but Derek might wake
up and I wouldn't be able to explain myself. He would
think I'm crazy. And he'd be right.

Obviously I can't fall back to sleep. Not with thoughts like these rolling over in my head. Even when I wake up safe in my bed, I can't let it go. This is awful. Isn't this what happens with split personalities? The evil takes over without the other's consent? I just need to know what is happening to me.

The other morning I was driving and I heard some banging from the trunk. I immediately pulled over, so I could free whoever was being held captive in my trunk. Trembling, I opened the trunk, bracing myself for whatever I was about to find.

It was my golf clubs rolling over when I made a turn. I am officially losing my mind. People joke about it all time. "Oh! I swear I'm losing my MIND! I forgot so-and-so's birthday!" I really am losing my mind and it has nothing to do with forgetting a birthday.

During the day, when I see images, I blink them away. They don't last long, but I'm left feeling confused and dumbfounded thinking, "What the hell was that?!" It's like someone showing me a picture of a person being burned, cut, or beaten, and then I choose to look away. Ick. It's so gross.

I usually have to look around my office or around a room to wipe it away like an etch-a-sketch. If I keep my eyes busy enough, then I won't be able to focus on my mind's image.

During the day, I'm able to clear it out. Nightmares are a different story. I don't have the knowledge or willpower to stop it while I'm sleeping. So I spiral into a nightmare until my panic attack wakes me up. I'm convinced I stop breathing when I have nightmares. I wake up gasping for air.

Un-Perfect

It's disappointing to see what my mind will produce when I'm not policing it. I didn't realize I had to work so hard to be good.

June 28, 2001

The images used to come and go, leaving me feeling (mostly) normal in between. Now I don't seem to have that in-between reprieve. Lately between the images, I'm stuck seeing myself in a different light.

I tie the images together with one constant thought: "I am evil."

I wouldn't have these thoughts if I were a good person. Therefore, I'm bad. Good people don't have these thoughts. Why didn't I understand this concept until now? I must have been in denial. Bad people think bad thoughts. I'm bad. I understand that now.

I'm rotten to the core and no one seems to understand this but me. They keep giving me compliments, "Kelly, you are so awesome. You're so positive. I want to be like you!"

People want to be like me. I cannot believe this. Why on earth would anyone want to be like me?

Each compliment has the opposite effect because it makes me feel manipulative. I sit at my desk while someone asks how it is that I'm so happy all the time. I float on the compliment for a bit, little butterflies under my feet, but then I crash. Because a few hours later, I will walk down the hall and smile at someone and out of the blue I will think, "What would she look like if she was shot in the head?" I blink the thought away, and say, "Hey, have a great morning!"

Jekyll and Hyde have nothing on me.

I don't think I was born pure and sweet like Parker. She reminds me of everything I'm not. Sweet, loving, open, beautiful. I reflect back the opposite. Evil, self-hatred, closed, repulsive. A wicked mirror I can no longer stand to see.

I'm convinced I'm a daughter of Satan. This seems totally insane even as I write this in my journal. I understand that. I'm reading the sentence and it looks crazy, but it is how I feel. I know it seems far-fetched and most people probably don't experience this feeling of belonging to something so evil. And I'm glad for them. In fact, I wish I were one of those people. I wish I wasn't the devil's daughter, but I truly believe that I have been called upon to create destruction.

If someone said, "Oh I see, you're Satan's daughter, living down there on the corner of Hell and Hell? Is that the right Satan?" that would sound crazy. Words don't describe it. It's a communication, an understanding, in my heart and soul. It's an unspoken truth and the experience is literally, out of this world. There is a voice that whispers to me, "You know I know the truth. You were born to be evil."

It's not like I'm walking around, slapping at the side of my head and yapping out loud to this communication. This voice is of the heart. I have

Un-Perfect

beautiful pockets of peace where I can ignore it. Sometimes I forget to act out a character and I laugh at funny things. I like those times when I forget to put on an act and I just AM. I'm just me without pretending anything.

June 29, 2001

While I'm dealing with this crazy shit, I'm also dealing with normal things like bedtime. I argue with Derek about when Parker should go to bed.

I push for 8:00 so he and I can have time together. He likes to stretch it out until 9:30 or 10:00 because we both work and should have as much time with her as possible.

"Kelly, she's only small once. What is wrong with snuggling with our daughter on the couch while we watch TV?"

Apparently nothing is wrong with it and thanks for making me feel like a prick for suggesting it.

I take this personally. He obviously doesn't care to spend alone time with me. *I'm* having a hard time being alone with me, so I get it, but I would think my husband would want to connect with me. He's even rejecting me before realizing how evil I really am. Ouch, that hurts.

I have a lot of roles to play and the role of "wife" was not exchanged for the role of "mother". It was simply added to numerous other roles, such as daughter, sister, friend, and employee. I have a hard time integrating all of them, but at least I haven't forgotten about being a wife too.

It's the million-dollar question, isn't it? How to balance selfishness with selflessness? How does a parent carve out personal time without feeling like an asshole? There is only so much of me to go around and a lot of times I'm skimming a little off the top on all my positions in order to attempt balance. That's when everyone is let down and I walk around feeling like a total loser.

I can't please everyone, but I sure as hell wear myself down to the bone giving it my best shot. If I make everyone on this planet happy, then that sends a message loud and clear to Satan: Take this job and shove it.

June 30, 2001

I feel like my head is dealing with a sucker punch over and over again. I never see it coming. Today I was playing with Parker, watching her giggle with crayons and then I thought, "What if she fell off the deck? Her little body would lying in the grass and I would accidentally move her, not knowing she broke her tiny neck, and I'd make it worse. She probably wouldn't be paralyzed if I hadn't moved her." But wait, that didn't even happen. I'm crucifying myself for paralyzing my daughter and she's not paralyzed. She's sitting in front of me coloring in a book. She's laughing and I'm worried about the possibility of her being paralyzed.

It's like someone is making me watch horror movie clips with all my loved ones in the starring roles. I don't have

Un-Perfect

the luxury of putting my hands over my face and watching through splayed fingers. It's all happening behind my eyeballs. It's impossible to look away.

I hate gory, horror movies. I take it so much further than anyone else in the theatre. To an extent, I take it seriously. I think about it for days. Years.

In the 80's my friend Shannon made me watch "Faces Of Death" and to this day I think about these little monkeys that were smacked on the head with a hammer in a restaurant so people could eat their brains. How can anyone forget an image like that? It's horrible. I can only imagine what those monkeys were thinking and how their tiny bodies were trapped under the table while people beat them. That is truly insane and cruel.

It's been almost twenty years and I'm still just as upset today as I was when I was fifteen. I have a hard time breathing when I think of those monkeys.

I can't imagine having my body trapped under a table unable to cover my head with my arms while someone bashes it in.

Actually, it's kind of how I feel lately.

Will I be thinking of this stuff when I'm ninety years old? Lying on my deathbed saying, "Save the monkeys!" I can see it now, Parker will be kneeling next to me holding my hand saying, "Oh here we go again with the fucking monkeys."

July 1, 2001

I think dandelions get a bad rap. They work so

damn hard to be beautiful, even going so far as sprouting yellow "petals", but they're never good enough. Everyone thinks they're useless and ugly.

Why? Because someone labeled them a weed.

They're so desperate to be seen they are even poking up through sidewalk cracks. "Please see me!" No one sees them. They just walk all over them. Or worse, pull them out of the ground, roots and all.

7/2/01 Sunday Muffins at Mom's

I sat at the counter while Dad read the paper and I said, "I'm so stressed out. I hate it." He said, "Well, then don't be stressed out."

Dad is so practical. I remember as a kid I'd say, "Ow, Dad my wrist hurts when I twist it like this." He'd reply, "Well, then don't twist it." That's his world. If I told him I was thinking I'm the daughter of Satan he'd say, "Well, if it bothers you, then don't think that way." His life is that easy.

Some people go through life without much thought about anything. It's not meant to be an insult, it's a gift. A gift to flow with life and know that all is well. Like Derek.

Un-Perfect

Yesterday I played the game. "What are you thinking NOW?!? Right now. Quick!?" He looked up from his book and said, "I'm thinking I'd like to read my book without my wife interrupting me." Never a bad thought in that man's head. Ever. It's fascinating to me.

Others, like me, are seekers. Things don't slide by me without interrogation, scrutiny and questioning. I need to see 360 degrees of each and every thing that touches my life before I embrace it, understand it and live with it.

I would love to be like Dad (and Derek) in the way that if he doesn't like something, he changes. When he was in his 30s he decided he didn't like working for a boss, so he bought his own franchise store selling tires. He sees life without panic or worry.

What a beautiful thing that would be.

Everything in my life seems to be earned with an anxiety attack. I'm pushing and prodding and turning and forming. But my father? Things float by and he slowly sips his coffee while deciding if he wants to take part in it or not. Maybe he will, maybe he won't. He makes a decision and that's that. No regrets. It's all good.

It's not that way for me. It would be like jamming a circle into a square. It would be painful for me to let everything go and just BE. What would happen? Dad would say, "Same thing as the day before."

And it *is* a waste of time. All this crazy thinking. I know this. So how can I stop?

July 3, 2001

For the first time in my life, I'm not worried about what anyone thinks of me. It's like taking off that dentist bib when you get x-rays. That heavy, lead-filled bib on my chest is gone.

What was I protecting myself from anyway? It feels so good to let it go. I move through experiences without any worry and anxiety. I am who I am. I know I'm bad. So?

I don't care if anyone compares me to my perfect family anymore and sees that I don't match. It's obvious I don't fit in, so why worry about it? It's not a secret. I don't belong with the beautiful people.

Who cares? I don't anymore. It's so weird, like my soul is filled Novocain. I don't give a shit about what anyone thinks of me for the first time in my life and I like it. Nothing affects me.

Un-Perfect

But on the flip side, I'm also numb to happiness. Yesterday, Parker was running around in her tutu and I knew that it should have made me smile, but it didn't. I smiled, but it wasn't real.

I'm becoming totally disconnected from everyone in my life. I don't feel joy, anxiety or pain. I don't care - and it makes me feel incredibly powerful. Nothing can hold me back. I haven't felt this powerful in my entire life.

Does evil come easily to everyone, or just me? Does everyone on this planet work hard against temptation to do bad things and struggle to do what's right? Or is everyone naturally good and I'm the only one feeling that it would be easier to be bad?

I'm trying not to kill myself, yet all these other people take their lives for granted. They don't even think about breathing. They pretend to be happy and then criticize everyone else. Is anyone really connected or are they all just jealous and scratching at each other's status symbols? That stuff doesn't matter and they don't see it. We could all die any minute and they're worried about driving a Saturn instead of a Lexus? Give me a break.

There is such disconnect between life and death. No, wait a minute, not life and death, LIVING and death. People have life, but they're not living. I'm on the cusp of killing myself and they're spending precious time bragging about designer jeans. That is not living.

You can't tell me their souls traveled all the way from heaven to see if their ass looks good in jeans. It's not fair that I will have to extinguish my light to save theirs.

I know it doesn't seem like it, but I'm trying to really *live* and feel and love and truly be here. I'm just experiencing technical difficulties in my head that is preventing progress. I want to love and be good and live my life, but my head is not cooperating right now.

Still, I have to believe this is temporary and will go away. I've always loved people, so this negative reaction to the mass population has to be a symptom of whatever is happening in my head. It's temporary. It has to be, because I don't want to do anything bad to anyone else and I don't want to kill myself in order to prevent that.

The only option is to get good again..

July 4, 2001

I **am** capable of remembering sweet things. I picked up my old journals to try and remind myself that I haven't always been like this. I used to live without thoughts of being demonic and cursed with a split personality.

Sunday December 8, 1986My boyfriend came over tonight and after he kissed me he said, "Love you." I said, "You DO???" He said, "Yeah, can't you tell?"

It is so weird to have someone other than my parents tell me that they love me!! I mean, I know that my family loves me, but they HAVE to because it's like the Family Rules.

But he doesn't have to and he does anyway! This is SO COOL!!!!!

Un-Perfect

I remember that feeling of being wrapped in someone's adoration and totally intoxicated with butterflies. I was sixteen experiencing first love and free of all of this heavy, horrible stuff. I was sweet and innocent once. It feels really good to know that I haven't always been evil and bad.

So if I was good before all this shit hit the fan, then that is the core of who I really am. I have been sweet and good for more years than I have been bad and shameful, which makes this is a temporary thing then.

June 6, 1999

We've been trying to get pregnant, but it's not working. I know, I know, it takes some people a long time, but I just thought we would be lucky.

It's been months and months and nothing is happening. What if we can't have kids?

I would never have a child come to me when he/she scraped a knee, or show me their favorite birthday present, or tuck my child into bed.

It's so sad.

We would adjust, of course. The hardest step in life is to find someone to love and have that someone return it. I thank my lucky stars that Derek and I found each other. I'm grateful for that, but I want to have a baby.

I just know I'm meant to be someone's mom. I'm crying while writing this because it hurts my chest to lose out every month we try.

I feel like I grieve a loss every twenty-four days, even though there hasn't been anyone to lose yet. It sounds ridiculous, but every month I attach my hope and love to someone I haven't met yet and then it goes away. It hurts my heart to lose hope.

Wow, I was sad about not getting to this place and now that I'm here, I'm too broken to enjoy it. That seems a little unfair. But I like seeing that I was a person that hoped and loved. My thoughts were gentle and sweet once. And this is relatively recent, so I haven't been fighting these thoughts for too long then, have I?

Or have I always had these thoughts floating in the back of my mind and now I'm just paying attention to them? No, that's not right. I know I haven't envisioned my father hanging from a noose before this. So this is new and started happening recently.

And if there's a beginning, then there is an end.

There is an end to this.

July 5, 2001

I was driving to the grocery store this morning and out of nowhere I thought of Parker's car seat falling out of the door and tumbling onto the freeway. She would still be strapped in and there wouldn't be time for the car behind me

Un-Perfect

to slam on its brakes.

I imagined her body getting smashed under the wheels of a car. Her little arms would tear right off and all the parts of her body would be sprinkled on the freeway, like a ripped-up doll.

Epileptics say they can feel a seizure coming because they'll start to taste something like metal or their mouth will go numb. I have no prep time. There is no preview. These thoughts slam into my head without any warning.

It's not fair. I don't have time to protect myself and get my boxing gloves on. And what am I fighting anyway? I shouldn't be fighting anything. I was just going to the grocery store like every other mom on the planet.

I looked in the rearview mirror to remind me that it didn't happen. My heart was banging against my ribs and I couldn't exhale. I repeated over and over again, "It is not real. It is not real. It is NOT REAL".

Parker was kicking her feet and smiling at me, totally oblivious of my wicked imagination. Thank God she doesn't understand what her mommy is thinking. I'm betraying her trust with these thoughts.

What mother thinks these thoughts? My daughter is the sweetest person I have ever known. My heart melted and I started crying. I feel. I'm not numb after all and it

Kelly Nordstrom

feels good to feel.

As I drove, tears rolled down my cheeks under my sunglasses. I would be so embarrassed if someone saw me crying in my car. What is wrong with me?

I need some kind of help, but where? I lied on my depression test for the second time at the OB/GYN office. But I lied because it's not quite right. Something else is making me depressed. I'm not just depressed out of the blue. I'm depressed (and terrified) of my imagination. My imagination is making me sad. I thought imagination was supposed to be a beautiful thing?

I checked "No" for all of the questions, except the "difficulty sleeping" question because I could blame that one on Parker.

Lack of joy: No. (yes)

Feelings of shame, guilt or inadequacy: No. (hell yes, so much that I'm choking on all of it)

Severe mood swings: No. (yes, but I pretend that everything is fine even when I'm full of rage because I don't want to scare anyone or have my husband leave me)

Difficulty bonding with baby: No. (yes, how can I bond with a baby that hated me for her first year of life and now asks daddy to sing her bedtime songs instead of mommy and wants mommy to "go away"? I do love her though. With all my heart.)

Un-Perfect

Withdrawal from family and friends: No. (And I really do mean "No" on this one. I see them because I want their happiness to rub off on me)

Thoughts of harming yourself or the baby: No. (yes, but I don't want to be committed into a padded room with medication jammed down my throat, have my daughter taken away from me, and have my husband divorce me)

Difficulty sleeping: Yes. (yes, but not because Parker has a cold and kept me awake, it's because I'm afraid I'll sleepwalk and suffocate her without being aware of it)

And now they gave me a pamphlet that has information about psychosis:

Postpartum psychosis treatment: Postpartum psychosis requires immediate treatment, often in the hospital.

Symptoms: Delusions or strange beliefs, hallucinations, feeling irritated, hyperactivity, decreased need for or inability to sleep, paranoia and suspiciousness, rapid mood swings, difficulty communicating at times.

When your safety is assured, a combination of medications — such as antidepressants, antipsychotic medications and mood stabilizers — may be used to control your signs and symptoms. Sometimes electroconvulsive therapy (ECT) is recommended as well. During ECT, a small amount of electrical current is applied to your brain to produce brain waves similar to those that occur during a seizure. The chemical changes triggered by the electrical currents can reduce the symptoms of depression, especially when other treatments have failed or when you need immediate results.

Something is wrong with me, but I don't understand what it is. I'm not paranoid or talking to make-believe people, so I'm free of psychosis. But I FEEL psychotic instead of depressed. I feel like I'm losing my mind.

I'm not understanding the hospital part. If I choose to drive myself to the hospital, do I walk into the ER? And then, in front of possibly a seven-year-old standing in line with a broken arm, I'm supposed to say, "I'm here because I don't like my imagination?"

I'm fairly certain that everyone in line will think, "My kid needs seventy-five stitches and you're having 'bad thoughts'?" I'm thinking they'll have a bad thought of wanting to slap me.

So let's say I get through the line without getting slapped or kicked by an angry adult. Then what happens? I sit in the waiting room next to someone bleeding out of their eye sockets and I'm there because I'm not liking the way I think lately?

Picture the two of us sitting next to each other in the ER. Honestly, it seems ridiculous to me. I cannot imagine how this all plays out. So I get called into a room and *then* what? I don't have a broken arm. I'm not bleeding. So I sit in one of those rooms next to all these people dying of heart attacks and strokes? I'm already surrounded by thoughts of death, I can't possibly be around it actually happening in real life. I might flip a lid.

But let's say I don't flip a lid and they admit me to a room, possibly a

Un-Perfect

padded one.

The pamphlet indicates that a combination of medications may be used to control my signs and symptoms. And possibly electroshock therapy. Good Lord, I can't picture anything other than being strapped down with a bunch of people jamming needles, electrodes and medication into my body. I'd be Jack Nicholson in "One Flew Over The Cuckoo's Nest", with nurse Ratchet turning me into a lobotomized, catatonic body.

I can't possibly volunteer to enter a world more terrifying than the one I'm already living in.

And they make the treatment plan sound like it's their decision, not mine. It doesn't say anywhere on this pamphlet that nothing will be used without my consent. And you know how many sheets of paper you sign when being admitted into a hospital, so one of them probably has some fine print that signs away my consent.

I cannot and will not ever hand my own authority over to anyone else. I'm still aware of what is happening to me and as long as my awareness is intact, I cannot allow another person to make decisions for me. It is not possible. I'm already uncomfortable with how much control I've lost. I cannot give up any more of it.

This whole process makes me bite the insides of my cheeks as I consider how this treatment plan would roll out. Angry welts rise to receive healing.

At least something in me is getting better.

DEREK

7/6/01

For Fourth of July we went to the capital to watch fireworks. Parker hates fireworks, I hate crowds, and Kelly was panicking about a stranger stealing Parker.

Ever try walking across a hundred people's blankets with a stroller, toddler, backpack, dolly, blanket, half-eaten turkey leg and water bottles?

It sucks.

July 8, 2001

I could wire a bomb to a bus if I wanted to. I don't want to, but I could. Anyone could. There are countless ways to harm people. How is everyone going to work and coming home every single day?

It's amazing that people walk through the doors to their home every evening unscathed. And ungrateful. They don't even understand they're lucky someone didn't wire their bus with a bomb. Don't they understand they're lucky to be alive?

This thinking is new and I hate it. I'm sorry. I'm so sorry for being me. I want to be someone else, but I'm stuck being me, thinking these thoughts.

How do we all live every day? Do other people consider what it would be like to end another person's life? Think about it. We all drive down highways

Un-Perfect

and the only reason we don't kill each other is because of yellow dashes. A yellow fucking dash. That's it. All you have to do is cross some paint and lives would be lost. It's that easy.

Am I the only one that thinks it's a little juvenile to paint some dashes and expect everyone to obey this rule? Can't we arrive at a resolution that is a little more innocuous? Cement beams would be appropriate on a two-lane highway to prevent freaks like myself from inching over the line. It's like colic of the mind. I can't help thinking these thoughts.

It's frightening to think there may be more of my kind walking around in this world with these kinds of thoughts running the show. At least I have control over my actions. No harm done, except in my own head. I can't say the same for the other nut jobs walking around. I mean, can it get *worse*? Is that why we see people on the news doing freaky things? Are they just like me, but with the dial turned a little bit more to the right?

What if one day I look in the trunk of my car and there really *is* a dead body in there?

I'm even finding it difficult to eat meat because it reminds me of a body that has been cut up. Is that what my body would look like if someone had me for dinner? Ick. I feel nauseous when someone eats steak. It's literally a slab of meat. I have to think the cow can still feel the pain. It's not even disguised as anything other than their body. Don't even go there with ribs. That is insane. For God's sake, the bone is still there. The body is still partially intact! It is dismembered and put on a plate. Talk about feeding a nightmare. That's perfect material to rise up and torture me while I sleep.

Anyway, these quickie "mind rapes" that I'm forced to endure are unbearable. I hate them. I will be sitting at lunch and then I see a baby in the oven. I'm always left a little abused and confused. "What just happened?" I almost want to ask the person sitting across from me if she just saw that. "Did

Kelly Nordstrom

you just see a baby in the oven?" Try eating your salad after seeing that.

I don't want to kill myself, but it's becoming evident that there is no other way. You know how fire has a back-draft? It's a situation which can occur when a fire is starved of oxygen and if oxygen is re-introduced by opening a door to a closed room, combustion can restart - often resulting in an explosive effect as the gases heat and expand. Back-drafts often surprise firefighters, regardless of their level of experience.

I'm a mental firefighter. I just need to stop opening the door to a closed room and allow the fire to die out on its own without oxygen. The images explode and recede, only to leave me with an anxiety attack. And then I'm normal again (except for the part that I'm the devil's daughter of course).

The intensity and frequency of these thoughts are increasing and I don't know how much more I can take before I have to end the thoughts.

And the only way to end the thoughts, unfortunately, is to end **me**.

July 9, 2001

I'm normally not a Nine Inch Nails rocker-goth chick, but I heard the song "Hurt" today and it resonates with me so completely I have to wonder if Trent Reznor is my long lost brother.

Music has a way of seeping into my bones and making me feel less alone. Derek just listens to the melody and enjoys the sound of it, whereas I bring the song into my soul if it's applicable. And this one is applicable.

At some point everyone I know will go away in the

Un-Perfect

end because I can't relate to anyone authentically. I will let everyone down and make them hurt; I'm wicked but they trust me anyway.

Wearing a crown of shit on a liar's chair full of irreparable broken thoughts describe me perfectly. Everyone around me lives their lives while I sit in a psychotic purgatory. I am living in hell while the world still spins.

I don't know what is wrong with me. Inside my head I'm shouting to the world, WHAT IS WRONG WITH ME??? WHAT IS HAPPENING TO ME!?? I am really scared. Of myself. That's pitiful.

My nightmare last night was unbearable. I kicked the shit out of this woman until she died. I was in a complete rage. Then I panicked because I didn't know what to do with the body, so I put her in the garage and hoped Derek wouldn't find out because then I would go to jail and everyone would know my secret. This morning, I couldn't help it, I peeked around the garage a bit to make sure it wasn't real. I know it's not real, but I'm soaking in guilt and panic anyway.

July 10, 2001

Last night, Derek and I were sitting at the counter. I said, "What about RIGHT NOW! What are you thinking?" He said, "I'm wondering why you do that thing with your cheeks."

"Do what?"

"I don't know, it looks like you're grinding your

teeth or something."

"Oh, I bite the insides of my cheeks. Don't you do that?"

"No, it would hurt. Why would I hurt myself?"

"I don't know. You mean, people don't pinch themselves or bite their cheeks or cut their gums around their teeth?"

"What are you talking about, cutting the gums around your teeth?"

"Well, when I was kid, I would take my fingernail and kind of shred up the gums around my teeth, but... What? Why are you looking at me like that?"

"Well, it's a little fucked up that you cause physical pain to yourself. I don't get it."

"I thought everyone did this kind of stuff. Don't you do anything like that? You scratch at your cuticles, I've seen you do that."

Yes, Derek plays with his cuticles, but he doesn't scrape them until they bleed. He's not in pain. I actually *like* that the insides of cheeks are in burning pain when cut them with my teeth.

I like feeling the bruised bumps in a row and I usually try to make the bumps into a perfect line across my cheek. I consider it unsuccessful when one of the bumps falls below the others and ruins the perfection. If I played with my cuticles like Derek, I'd be pulling the skin out from around the nail until it's a

Un-Perfect

perfectly straight line around my nail bed. I'm guessing he doesn't do this.

This is surprising to me. I didn't realize this was something that only select people do. I thought everyone would pinch or test the pain boundaries of their bodies like I do. I don't like learning that it's not normal, or it's "special behavior" to help establish control or relieve anxiety. I've simply never given much thought to it because I didn't think it was an unusual thing to do.

I don't want to be weird. I'm already a mental mess. Why does Derek get to be normal and perfect and a great parent and I'm all screwed up? I'm so jealous of him. He has his life in order without even trying. He's a great dad without reading the books.

I keep reminding myself that I'd rather have him be a good parent than a bad one because when I go away then Parker will be taken care of, but at the same time, it sucks knowing they don't need me. It's almost embarrassing wondering why I'm still around.

July 11, 2001

Where is the OFF switch? Shut the world off. I'm so ashamed. Everyone knows how to move in this world but me. Why am I so lost when I have what everyone dreams of?

I'm a wife, mother, friend and sister, yet I can't feel it. It's like a ghost trying on clothes. What's the point?

I'd rather jump from a building than succumb to these horrific thoughts. I never thought I believed in hell, but it's right here in my head.

If I kill myself then that is one less evil person in

this world. My daughter will be safe. My husband will marry someone better than me. People can go on with their lives comparing cars, clothes, and bank accounts without me.

But I can't imagine Derek with anyone else but me. Would he re-marry if I went away? What if his new wife was controlling? Oh great, this already sucks and I'm not even gone. No one is ever going to be able to step into my role and fill my spot like a substitute teacher.

I can't hand over a syllabus and explain that the leftover chicken in the fridge needs to be thrown out in two days. I can't describe how to kiss Parker's bellybutton and if you listen to her chest, it will remind you of the sonograms when I was pregnant. I can't launch out of the grave to say, "No, don't talk in a baby voice to Derek, he hates it when grown women talk like babies, talk to him like..."

What if this new wife yells at Parker? I can't "un-cremate" myself and slap this faux mom across the face.

Let's face it. Dead is releasing control and frankly, I'm a big fan of control. I thrive on it. Maybe that's why this whole evil gig is so difficult. I have no control over these thoughts. They just march right into my head, totally uninvited. They're so rude. To say it is frustrating is an understatement.

There is no rhyme or reason to the intensity or frequency of the thoughts, other than rest. If I sleep well for a few days, they seem to be less frequent. I love those days. They remind me that I'm good.

July 12, 2001

It's not fair. I've been sleeping better, but I was

Un-Perfect

mentally bitch-slapped while standing in line at Target. Just out of the blue, I wondered what it would be like to shoot someone in the head.

I want to be normal like everyone else in that line. I've been sleeping better the last few nights and I haven't had a nightmare. I thought I was getting over this and now it's back. It pisses me off. It's not even scary today, just annoying and stupid. I'm so frustrated.

What is this and when will it go away?

July 13, 2001

I'm jealous of my daughter. What kind of mother is jealous of her own child? I'm jealous because she has such an open heart, ready to give affection and I've worked hard to close that valve shut and be stoic.

So I'm forced to watch Derek's face beam with happiness when she hugs him. I've never seen his face look like that with me. And I hear them from the kitchen laughing together and I know their arms are wrapped around each other.

What is he trying to prove, that he's a better parent than me?

Yeah, I get it. He's outshining me in the Parent

Competition. If we kept score it would be a thorough ass-kicking with Derek strong in the lead. It would be a major shut-out because I don't believe I've scored even one point.

I hate it. I hate that she's giving him more attention and affection that I ever have and I resent her for it. And I hate seeing it or trying to become a part of it because I'm all awkward, trying to put on a fake, silly façade.

And truly, I don't even want to be around them. She's reminding me of where I'm falling short. I don't hug my husband unless people are there to witness it to prove that I'm a good wife. I'm a good wife on *paper*. I hug and kiss him so other people can see that I hug and kiss him and tell me that I'm a great wife. See?

I'm a Paper Wife. I'm good only on paper when doing a checklist:

Fit body: Check

Laughs and jokes: Check

Sex twice a week: Check

Social at parties: Check

Everyone remembers that when they were dating. You would come home from a bombed date and wonder where it went wrong. Then scratch it down on paper: "He has money, great body, he's polite, has great friends." And then wonder, "Why am I not in love with this person?"

It's because he's a Paper Date. He's good only on paper and you sensed that there is nothing underneath all the checkpoints. You couldn't feel his heart and soul because he shut that valve off. This is why I'm baffled that Derek still wanted to be with me. I've never been heavy on the affection and I like being

Un-Perfect

unemotional, so I don't know how he saw the good stuff inside of me. I'm grateful for it, but I don't know how he found it in me when I can't even be sure I have it.

The good stuff. Love, care, tender feelings, empathy, consideration. I don't know if these things exist inside of me and now I have my daughter throwing a spotlight on it.

She's closer to him than me and I've had ten years with him. She's only had one, but seems to have trumped all my efforts. Once again, I'm falling short. I know that mothers would be proud of a daughter that loves and cares for her dad, but I'm threatened by it. What mother competes with her own daughter for her husband's attention? Shameful.

Most mothers would love for their husband to have such a sweet bond with their daughters. What is wrong with me? I'm also competing with Derek for Parker's attention and she always chooses Derek to win. He gets hugs and I get "No! Go!" Then I pout. I actually pout like a child.

I don't know how to release the competition and not let every single thing reflect on me. Derek hugging Parker has nothing to do with me, so why am I making it about me? I'm a narcissist in the highest order. How do I allow other people to just be who they are instead of who *I want them to be*? Because I'm scared to death she'll choose Derek as the better parent and I'll be kicked to the curb. That's why.

I want to be the Chosen Parent. The Favorite. I don't want to think this way, but I can't stop it. He's the Favorite and I'm the pouty teenager standing in the kitchen with her arms linked across her chest so no one can get into her heart. Something is not right.

July 14, 2001

I'm convinced I have a split personality. I'm exhausted, and I wonder if it's because my evil sidekick kills people at night when I sleep. And since split personalities don't know what the other "person" is doing, I'm only left with what I think are nightmares.

How do I know that my nightmare didn't really happen? I want to hide the knives and scissors in the cabinets, but Derek will ask why I did that, so I have to leave them on the counter. They just sit there, all sharp and menacing. Knives stab people and I hate thinking about people being harmed. Scissors can slip off the counter and accidentally cut people. I hate seeing sharp things. Even paper edges. They slice right through skin and it's so painful.

The other end of the spectrum is just as threatening. Pillows suffocate people. Cotton balls can be bad because Parker could try eating them and suffocate. I read that a child drank baby oil and died, so now I hide the baby oil. I used to leave it out and slather it on after showers, but not anymore. What if Parker kissed my leg and got baby oil on her lips? I knew about hiding cleaning supplies, but Baby Oil? Nothing is safe.

Un-Perfect

I sit at my desk waiting for the local news to show me caught on tape beating someone to death or killing someone. And honestly, I will be just as surprised as everyone else when the police come to get me. I'm not in control of this evil part of me and no one will understand that.

Hell, I don't even understand it, so I don't expect anyone else to believe it. It's still unbelievable to me that I have a split personality. But I can't deny it. There is something or someone else occupying my life and it is awful. I have no control over it.

July 15, 2001

Everyone is capable of doing horrific things. They may not do anything about it, but they are capable of it. It's the spectrum of humanity, from black to gray to white. Evil to good. We're capable of everything on the spectrum. That's why all these people are outraged by Andrea Yates. She reminds them of what they could do if they didn't have a healthy mind to prevent them from doing it.

People are not doing catastrophic things because they have healthy minds to police their behavior. That healthy mindset makes them cringe and become outraged. But just because they're outraged, doesn't mean they're not capable of it.

A healthy mindset is like the dashes on a highway. It reminds you not to cross the lines because you will hurt another person. No one questions it because people with healthy minds support and embrace other people.

It's actually a very nice gesture.

The next time your faith in humanity is lacking, just remember that people are not crossing those lines on the highway because they value your life.

Every person on this planet is capable of physically killing another person. That's a fact. Every person is also capable of helping another person. That's a fact. We're all from the same divine soup, God, whatever you want to call it. We're all from the same place, therefore we all have the same basic capabilities to contribute to this planet. Good or bad.

Either we choose to embrace this world and make it better because of what we put in it, or we choose to destroy it.

Every person gets a canvas on which to paint their story. Currently I'm a little screwed up, but I do understand that if I misbehave, my canvas goes down in flames. There are no replacements.

Even though I'm capable of doing horrific things, I choose to be good. No one else should have to suffer because of this hell in my head. It's all mine.

7/16/01 Sunday Muffins at Mom's

Today I went alone because I wanted to have time to myself without pouring eighty-five glasses of juice for Parker and changing her diaper.

Un-Perfect

I used to hate being away from her, getting a sick stomach if we were separated. Not anymore. The constant demands wear my patience down to a nub, then I feel guilty for blowing a gasket. I figured I should take a break and save myself from the guilt.

It felt so good to be me without a little person demanding to be picked up, asking for crayons, having a tantrum on the floor, getting syrup all over her clothes and even in her hair (I feel for guilty for saying that, so I guess I didn't escape the guilt after all).

I had full conversations with my parents and sisters and wanted to stay in that house forever. I didn't want to go home back to the place where I was such a failure.

Then again, the more my sisters talked about their lives, the more I felt discombobulated and confused. All my life I have felt like they set the bar a little too high. Everything falls into place for them (and even if it didn't, they would never complain about it). I'm such a whiner about everything. They were both noted in their yearbooks as "Sweetest" or "Nicest". My only mention was my school picture on page 86.

They had a combined party once when my

parents went on a trip. They made my sisters promise to take good care of me while they were away. Mom wanted me to stay with grandma, but I begged to stay home with my sisters. I pictured snuggling up on the couch watching movies together. Little did I realize, they were sixteen and twenty and ready to party.

It seemed like my sisters had a million friends. I walked around with an ashtray, asking people to watch their cigarettes. I was the Walking Worrywart, always making sure carpets were kept clean and people were behaving themselves.

People would slur, "Sheez so cute, jus like a 'lil mothrrr." I was also the beer runner for the drinkers in the basement, so I'd run upstairs to grab beers for everyone. They'd cheer when I arrived with an armload of Coors.

I did not like it. I wanted everyone to go home so I could tuck my twelve-year-old body into bed. Responsible beyond my years. This could be where my love of control began. People were crying to me about their boyfriends and warning me about school. The only thing I heard was, "Don't be like me." No worries there.

Un-Perfect

I later learned that Kari was so worried about everyone ruining the house that she called the cops and busted her own party.

But you get the idea. Everyone knows (and loves) my sisters. They have paved the golden path for me. Maybe it wasn't me doing all that work after all. It was them. All I have to do is put one foot in front of the other, yet I can't even get *that* right. I'm stuck stumbling around, confused about where to go next, while they keep taking risks and having everything perfect and pretty.

I know they don't intend for me to feel this way, but it's the way I'm wired to digest it. Other people may not care if their sister became the President of the United States, but I would hunker in her shadow with my arms crossed like an ungracious teenager.

Do all the babies of the family have this tendency or is it just me?

As I pondered this, Dad waltzed in, grabbed my shoulders and said, "How's my Sweetieheart? You want an omelet?"

I smiled a true smile and said, "I'm good and of course I want an omelet." And at that moment, I was good. I like being greeted with a shoulder squeeze.

As Mom changed the garbage she asked, "So, how's it going?" I put on a brave face for her and explained that everything was great and I was just so thankful there's no more screaming and everything was falling into place really well.

But the entire time I was speaking I couldn't take my eyes off that plastic bag. *An entire adult body would fit in there. I could fit in there. I could crawl in it and tie it from the inside – how long would it take for me to die? Would I try ripping it open?* I hate plastic bags. I hate them. Why wouldn't she just wait to change the garbage after I left? Who changes the garbage in front of their guests – it's rude. No one else at the counter was upset by looking at it. They weren't even concerned by the fact that it could kill me. I went to the bathroom so I didn't have to look at that huge plastic bag.

Anyway, I don't want Mom to think I'm failing. I couldn't even look her in the eyes, so I busied myself with grabbing a plate and silverware. Her knowing I'm failing is worse than me actually failing.

She always trusts that I'm doing my best. But what if my best isn't good enough? What

Un-Perfect

if she learns that she raised a satanic daughter that worries about death? That's a little rougher around the edges than getting a "C" in geography.

But then again, of course she knows I'm her satanic daughter. I'm convinced she adopted me. And if she knows I'm satanic, why did she change the garbage in front of me? To test me? To see if I'd freak out? Doesn't she understand that plastic bags could be a weapon of destruction? Of course she doesn't. She's not evil like me. She's a happy, normal person. God, I wish she were my real mom.

It's just so evident as I sit at the counter. Mom probably knew about my evil tendencies when she learned about my real parents. I'm guessing they were serial killers. I looked at the woman across the counter from me and knew that I can't ever let her down after all she's done for me.

I wish I could tell my parents about that man stalking me and plotting to take Parker, but I don't want them to worry. I hope that man, the kidnapper or my real father, would just attack me and be done with it. I don't like people looking at me from the shadows, staring at me. And I hate that he has a picture of Parker and me. Why did I agree to let him take our picture?

It's the waiting, the anticipation of knowing that something terrible is about to happen and I can't stop it. Why doesn't he just attack me and get it over with?

July 17, 2001

It's been said that it takes a village to raise a child. Where's my village? I can't reach out to anyone because they'll take my daughter away. Maybe I'm the only high maintenance, psychotic idiot that requires an entire village, but I do.

There. I said it. I need a village to help me, but I'm held hostage alone in this cell of my body because I'm scared that if I fess up about anything, Parker is going to go away.

And then people will tell horrible stories about how her mother is nuts and she'll disown me.

I want to be a good mom. I don't want to be a mom that is locked away for thinking this way. I need a village comprised of a nutritionist, psychiatrist, life coach, and physical trainer. I need a strong suit of armor to protect me against Satan. This all started after I had Parker - I should have left

Un-Perfect

the hospital with my posse, providing me with physical, emotional, and mental support. But that's not possible. The fucking hospital sent me home totally alone, and frankly incapable, of evolving into motherhood without a coach.

Going from non-mother to mother is a huge transition, not to mention that my body was crashing from a tornado of hormones. Yet no one gives a shit. Just because a million women do it every day, it's assumed that I'm fine. And sure, some women are fine. I hate them of course for succeeding at something I'm miserably failing at, but yes, some women are totally fine. Some women need a little help. And some women, like me, need an entire village of specialists.

But now it's too late because I'm too far gone. I certainly can't go to a support group and tell everyone that I'm considering suicide in order to save mass population from my destruction. I would be locked up before I can say, "Help me". I'm at the point now where I'd be punished if I tried to get help.

July 18, 2001

Some days are better than others, where I experience a lot of peace from my terrible imagination (or Satan – I can't figure out which). Today is one of them, which is why I'm a little more forgiving about how bad it sucks.

I run around the house with Parker, I push her in the swing in our backyard and grab her toes, I play board games with Derek and laugh. I like these little reprieves even though I feel like I'm faking.

Because if they knew what was going through my

head a few hours ago, they wouldn't believe that I'm playing Hide and Seek with Parker and tickling her belly.

It's so weird. One minute I'm convinced I'm Satan's daughter and the next minute I feel normal and think that's a crazy idea. To me, this confirms the idea of a split personality. I feel like if I waved the white flag and drove myself to a hospital, by the time I got there, my "good side" would come out and my disturbing images would be gone. This feeling of having a split personality scares me. Who is this other person that floats up when I'm not looking?

I don't like the idea of hosting a home for a crazy woman. I want to be all me. I don't want to share this life with a mental illness.

I can't seem to stop the thoughts so I've started "recycling" them as they come. I picture scissors cutting an image out and throwing it away in the garbage. Scissors and garbage bags. I use these items on purpose because it challenges me to use them for GOOD THINGS, instead of bad things. It makes me turn my thinking around.

Anyway, it's like dragging an icon to the recycle bin on my computer. Actually, it's exactly like that. I drag my shitty thought to the recycle bin in my head. I hope, hope, hope, that the image is somehow getting recycled into something cute and shiny. Balloons and rainbows for crisssake. Anything that doesn't involve blood or death would be a welcome snapshot at this point.

I drag the thought of checking my trunk for a dead body to the trash and remind myself that it is not real. Then twenty minutes later I'll wonder if my evil split personality was the driver of a hit and run last night while I was sleeping. I drag *that* thought to the trash and remind myself that it's not real. But I'm not so sure about that one. Why else am I so tired all the time? If I have a split personality and my evil sidekick was out on a killing spree every night, it would

Un-Perfect

explain why I'm so exhausted even when I don't have a nightmare.

It's incredible that I'm still going to work and getting anything done sans error. While I discuss a budget of $1,750,000, I'm throwing away an image of someone being stabbed and sliced. It's mental multi-tasking and it's incredibly difficult.

And I do it with a smile on my face, which is even more amazing.

So, unless there is a real life or death situation, I am completely absorbed in my own recycling program. A recycling of the mind.

DEREK

7/18/01

What am I thinking about RIGHT NOW?! I'm thinking Kelly can't make a decision to save her life.

It's so frustrating. Trying to decide where to go for date night is excruciating. I can't get a commitment on where to go, what to do, what she should wear, when the sitter should come and go...it takes effort not to get pissed.

Why do women ask what they should wear? Why does this question even exist? Nails in a coffin. There is no way I'm going to fess up and say, "Maybe your other jeans would be better." That would be sexual suicide.

Note: What is up with the cheek-biting? Why

would anyone purposely hurt themselves? Makes no sense. I don't get it. And as much as I know she's trying to stop the cheek thing, she's still doing it. Constantly. I don't dare say anything because I know she'll get mad, accusing me of pointing out that she's weird.

July 19, 2001

I don't like that anyone can see my routine. Now that I'm back to work, the man that took our picture knows where I work.

Sometimes I get off the bus a little early and take the skyway just to trip him up. I don't like bringing Parker to daycare every day at the same time so I try and go at different times in case someone is trying to learn my pattern.

I'm so glad when Derek's schedule gets erratic. If anyone is stalking my family, that will confuse them. But when he has a consistent schedule, someone can pin down our routine. They'll know when Parker and I are alone in the house and come in and kill us.

And besides being stalked, I have an imagination that seems to be stuck inside a haunted house.

Un-Perfect

How on earth am I able to connect with anyone? It's difficult to concentrate during "thought-slaughts". I usually try to pretend I'm looking for something in my notes or adjust my shoe. Sometimes I need to halt conversation and give me a godforsaken minute to recycle the thought of throwing someone down a stairwell. During meetings I will say, "Wait, can you repeat that? I want to make sure I'm understanding it correctly." They don't need to repeat it – I already heard what they said. I took notes on it. But as they repeat an idea, it buys me a few minutes to stare at my notes and recycle a heinous thought.

How do I see an image while someone is speaking to me? I guess it's like having a conversation with someone wearing a hideous Santa sweater with bells on it. You're trying to concentrate on the conversation, but as she's explaining the amazing Christmas deals at Target, you're thinking, *Why on earth is she wearing that hideous sweater? Why does that sweater have fucking bells on it? Is it a joke or a dare – is that why she's wearing it? How much would that sweater COST? Where is it even sold? How does a person even FIND such an ugly sweater?* And then you reply to her about the deals at Target saying, "Oh good! Thanks for the tip!" Bells. On a sweater. I've seen it.

It's relatively easy to carry on two conversations, one in your mind and one out loud. It's just that my "mind" conversation has become images instead of words.

We all think in dialogue. But lately my dialogue has become horrific, gory images. So instead of thinking, *I wonder what it would be like if a person was hit by a train?* I see it happening. I see bodies being dismembered and ripped apart, then wonder if anyone would notice the blood splattered on the sides of the cars. I imagine someone washing the blood off the sides of the cars. I'm not thinking in words, I'm thinking in pictures.

And Parker. Poor thing.

We play, but I'm so busy pretending to be normal and happy, that it's not real. I constantly worry about getting cancer. I worry about having a split personality and being adopted. I worry that she has cancer. I worry that Derek has cancer. I worry that she'll find a plastic bag and suffocate. I worry about everything.

I used to be so shocked and saddened by the images I would see, but now I just cut the picture out and recycle it. Just another bloody image. Nothing new, no big deal. I've become completely desensitized by the images. Oh sure, another person hanging from a noose. Seen that before. It doesn't bother me.

I don't know if that's good or bad. I guess good because I'm not letting these unreal images affect me, but bad because somewhere in this world, these things are probably happening and I don't care.

Unless it involves a child. Images like that are the most intense and truly interrupt my behavior. I have a hard time smiling over anything involving a child. If I'm at work and I get an intense image with a baby or child being harmed, I'll wait until the meeting or conversation is finished, then go to my desk and stare at the keyboard until I recycle it out.

Other times, I've gone to the bathroom with an anxiety attack and I wait it out until my heart stops pounding and the sweating stops. I've missed meetings because of this and people ask where I've been. I tell them my other meeting ran late. I'm technically not lying because I had a meeting of the mind that could not be postponed.

July 25, 2001

I want another baby. I can't explain why, but I have this pull to have another baby.

Maybe part of me recognizes that I didn't have these

weird thoughts when I was pregnant and I hope the hormones will get rid of it. Maybe part of me wants to see if I'm capable of having another baby without losing my mind. Maybe this is my way of telling the world that I'm here to contribute good things, not bad things.

Maybe it has nothing to do with anything going on in my head, but rather, I deserve to forge ahead with my life as my heart sees fit. I have more to give, more to create, more to love.

Without this second child, I will feel a void deep in the center of my being. Parker needs and deserves to have someone that will connect with her, a twin soul with whom she can bond. If anything, someone with whom she can commiserate because mommy is a little nutty.

Derek is on board. He just looked up at me from the floor where he was playing with Parker and said, "Really? Well, okay then. I love you." And that was that. We are officially trying for another baby. No more birth control pills.

July 29, 2001

I'm trying not to control when I get pregnant.

Part of me wants to barge into Derek's sperm tank

with a PowerPoint presentation to explain that I'll be ovulating soon, so they better get their racing shoes on.

The other part of me knows that it will probably take almost a year like it did with Parker, which will be best anyway since I'm still a little wacky in the head.

I just don't want to get to a place where I'm totally fine, then want another baby and have to wait a year. I don't like waiting and I definitely don't want to get to the point where I'm crying every month when I get my period. Been there. Done that. Don't want to do it again.

So I consider this kind of a pre-game for pregnancy. A warm-up for the real deal when it happens in about 10 months.

I'm not telling anyone we're trying because here's what will happen: Everyone will share their story about how easy it was for them to get pregnant.

When we were trying for Parker, I wanted to slap every woman that said, "I barely think about having sex and I get pregnant. I'm just a Fertile Myrtle!" Yeah, yeah, go fuck yourself. I had ten months of charting my period, taking my temperature, and having sex in stupid positions trying to get pregnant.

Plus, does anyone really care to know when people are trying to get pregnant? When someone tells me they're trying to get pregnant, I immediately picture the couple having sex and I don't *want* to be thinking about them having sex. It's like I'm held hostage in a mental threesome with them when I didn't want to be invited in the first place.

Un-Perfect

August 1, 2001

I went to the beach today with Parker. She was so cute in her little pink ruffled one-piece swimsuit and jean hat.

We were splashing around in the water and I walked out waist-deep. I tickled her belly and swished her around in the water, giggling and saying, "Swish! Swish! Swish!" She laughed so hard she got the hiccups. She would tip her head back, the sun beaming on her sweet chubby cheeks. Her blonde ringlets were floating in the water like a mermaid.

Hair floating in the water. What if she was face down floating in the water and all I could see was her hair? What if that happened and I couldn't get to her in time?

I immediately started walking to shore. She yelled, "Mommy! Swish!" No honey, no more swish. All I could think about was my ten measly fingers holding her ENTIRE LIFE. Oh my God, if those fingers let her go, she would drown and die and it would be my fault.

Something is horribly wrong with me.

Today I'm painfully aware there is no lifeguard to blow the whistle and save Parker from my thoughts. Today, my daughter was almost harmed. By me. Her mother. My God, she could have drowned! What was I thinking bringing her to the beach? She could have died. It could have happened.

206

Kelly Nordstrom

I could have let her go and I would have killed her. I can't handle that thought. It is beyond terrifying to me. I cannot breathe even as I write this. I can't breathe. I can't breathe. I can't breathe. Maybe I am dying. Maybe I'll just suffocate on my own terror and die.

But I'm still here. Breathing. Dammit.

What mother thinks these thoughts? Oh my God, what the hell is wrong with me? Why am I thinking these things? Who am I? What is happening to me?

This means that I cannot postpone my suicide any longer. I have to go before I hurt her. I don't want to die. I'm actually afraid to die. But I'm more afraid of hurting Parker. I only have ten fingers. What if they went numb for some reason and I couldn't hold her anymore? What if I had a heart attack while we were in water over her head? What mother takes her baby in water over her head? I can't believe how careless I am. I'm a horrible mother. What if I tripped on a rock and I slipped and let her go? So many things could have happened today and it would have been my fault.

The only way to stop these thoughts is to stop my life.

The panic I felt was like trying to save her from the jaws of a shark. Me. I'm the shark. I cradled her entire body against mine when we reached the shore and sat on our towels. We made it. We sat in the sand. Together. Safe.

That's when I asked a stranger to take our picture. I have to see what other people see when they look at me. Can they see the monster inside or not? Do I look normal? I don't feel normal. Do I still look like me? I'll get the pictures developed tomorrow or the next day. I don't expect to recognize the woman in the picture, posing as me.

I'm so scared to die. I'll put it off until I get this picture back. I may need it to give me strength to do what I need to do. It will remind me of why I need to go. I'm too irresponsible to have a baby. I love my daughter with every

Un-Perfect

cell in my body and will do anything to keep her alive and well. Even if it means the death of me.

DEREK

8/2/01

I'm not jealous of Kelly, I'm jealous of the time she gets to have with Parker.

Okay, I'm a little jealous of Kelly.

She has a job she loves and she actually has fun at work. C'mon, they serve *beer* at their company meetings. And every Friday off in the summer? I can't imagine.

Kelly is one of those lucky people that seem to have a horseshoe rammed up her ass. Jobs land in her lap, friends love her, and she just always seems to get what she wants.

I don't get why she ever worries about anything, because life always seems to cater to her.

I'm sorry, I'm sounding like a dick.

And I'm not, I swear.

I'm just jealous.

LIFE CHAPTER 3:
HEALING

Where do we find strength?

We look for it everywhere

Until we're forced to find it
In ourselves.

To contain our spirit and
give the self permission to
search the soul and reconstruct our being

Is a gift like no other.

Un-Perfect

"Grateful To Be Alive"

My journey to get better.

I remember trying to make my world heaven,

surrounding myself with only good, positive things,

so I could climb out of hell.

I finally started laughing again. REALLY laughing.

It felt so good to laugh again.

August 3, 2001

I got the picture back and it looks just like me. I'm shocked. We should look like two victims of my mind's assault, but instead we look like a happy mom and daughter playing at the beach.

No wonder everyone thinks I'm fine. I look fine.

I don't want to die. Today I'm going to live. I will do everything in my power to keep Parker alive, healthy and happy.

Yesterday was horrifying. I was awake with panic attacks all night... crumpled on the bathroom floor thinking it through. I couldn't breathe. I already felt like I died – I was floating again. When I have a panic attack, my breathing gets faster and faster like a propeller, then my vision gets narrow, and all I can think about is how to get out of my own skin. I don't want to be here, I want out, I want to get out of this body away from here, I want to be somewhere else but I don't know how to get there. I get thirsty and dizzy, like my body drops out into inky black space. Floating.

I sat against the cold tub and cried my face off. I considered removing the blades out of my razor and slitting my wrists, but that is not going to be my recovery plan. I didn't want to die, I just wanted to feel pain. I wanted to cut

Un-Perfect

my legs to see if I could feel pain, but I didn't. Instead I bit the insides of my cheeks. Physical pain pulls me out of a panic attack because it reminds me that I'm still here in this body. I didn't float off and die. I'm still here.

I don't know how yet, but I am going to beat this fucking condition to the ground. I am done being scared and terrified of my own head. It's ridiculous.

And what's really screwed up is that there were people on that beach looking crazier than me. One woman was wearing tube socks with sandals, paired with an obnoxious black and gold one-piece swimsuit. She looked certifiably nuts.

But I watched her and listened to her as I sat in the sand having a panic attack, after we made it back to shore. That woman's only concern in the world was whether or not her daughter had sunscreen on her shoulders. She was normal. I was not.

Passersby thought she was the crazy one. But little did those people know it was the one next to her that was filled with terror and horror. Me. The one in the Ralph Lauren, royal blue tankini. The one that was dressed appropriately with a big sunny, smile on her face. She's the one they should've been monitoring.

It's so weird. I don't look broken.

The world is trained to look at the physical nature of things like a fractured arm, thinning hair, and broken neck. We're accustomed to find and fix only things we can see and touch. What about a fractured spirit?

With an arm, you x-ray it and show the patient how well it healed. You can't x-ray a person's head to prove that all the psycho babble was removed. You can't grab a sickening image and remove it from their thinking.

I wish I had a physical ailment - in fact I've considered throwing myself down stairs so I could break a bone, but I'm too chicken. Instead, I just wish that I would get into a car crash. But I can't be the one to cause the crash because the guilt will sink me further into the hole. It has to be a lucky accident.

Instead, I live each day unscathed. Another reason I should be ecstatic. But I'm not.

I relate to women that have postpartum shit. Whether it's psychosis, I don't know. Maybe I'm schizophrenic, but I don't really think so. Maybe I'm just plain horrible. Maybe I'm bipolar. I'm not sure, but the postpartum stuff feels like it could be right. I didn't feel like this until after I had Parker. It HAS to be something postpartum.

While it's a relief I'm not alone, I really don't need the label of postpartum depression. The label is just an umbrella that covers hundreds, maybe thousands, of women like me. We're all huddled under it, trying to keep each other warm and strong, but we're still individuals. Our own stories, falling like raindrops out of the sky.

Are raindrops all the same? No. And neither are the women standing under the umbrella.

I have my own journey, my own choices and my own experience. If you served up my exact experience to another woman, she would probably digest it completely different than me. There is no right way to survive.

How dare anyone judge another person when they're dealing with catastrophe.

Today I'm committed to finding a way out of this mess. I'm going to survive and I'm not going to look back. I hope it's a postpartum thing. I don't want to be schizophrenic.

Un-Perfect

8/5/01 *Sunday Muffins At Mom's*

Through all my suffering and self-preoccupation, I forgot that if I commit suicide, children other than Parker will be hurt. I'm also a role model for my nephews Jake, Corey, and Ethan and my nieces Holly and Hanna. I've been so sucked into myself that I forgot that other people would be impacted too. Not to mention Derek, my parents, sisters, brothers-in-law, and friends.

Today was a combined party for Dad and Jake since their birthdays are so close together. We sang "Happy Birthday" and as they blew out their candles, I made my own wish. I looked down to the floor so no one could see me close my eyes. *I wish for everyone in this room, including me, to be healthy, happy and loved.* Then I opened my eyes and yelled a big "Woo Hoo!" since they blew out about 77 candles. Mom added their ages together and stuck them all in there like a big chocolate bonfire.

Parker had cake all over her face and in her hair. We didn't care. We'll give her a bath later. Today, it's all good. Eat the cake and ice cream. Laugh extra loud when a joke is funny. Today, I'm here. With my family. Derek looked over at me and winked while Parker fed him a bite of ice cream. Was all of this here last year and I just missed it?

Jake was front-and-center by his cake and we all crowded around him to take our family picture. My dad set the timer and made a run for it as it beeped. He yelled, "OKAY EVERYONE, SAY, 'ETHAN IS A SNOT NOSE!'"

It was a good day today. I didn't even allow it to be otherwise. As soon as any unwelcome thought came up I said, "Not today. You're not allowed in my head today."

I'm going to live, dammit.

August 6, 2001

I know I am not well, but I can't ask for support for fear my daughter will be taken away from me. I can't risk medication because if someone gets the dosage wrong or prescribes the wrong thing, I'm fucked.

If I go on medication, I'll convince myself that I can't live without it. The doctor will wean down the potency and I will make myself crazy wondering if I'm still crazy. I'll worry about each and every thought, panicking that it's coming back. I need to resolve this on my own because I can't risk having it

Un-Perfect

come back when I go off medication.

The healing needs to happen with me being me. Raw and real. I need to feel the changes and know they are happening because of who I am. I need the good in me to wash out the bad in me.

That is how it has to happen. It's how I roll. I need to do this alone. I can't have medication to blame for erratic behavior. Healing somehow needs to rise out of that crude, organic place that is seething with rage.

Me on medication would be like spreading pink frosting over a cake of rusty nails. I need to get into the bones of this fucking beast and heal its hurting wound.

I can't hang onto a pill for life because I will worry about the amount, demand higher doses, and probably begin taking two or three. Doctors would hate me because I'd be so high maintenance and I'd abuse the dosage.

Wait a minute, this never occurred to me, but apparently I have addiction issues. Okay. Well then. It's time to admit that I like prescription drugs. A pill for every ill. And then a little more for good measure.

There is no room for pretending that everything is perfect and dandy. I don't have that luxury – I've got to get real. NOW. Sometimes the truth hurts. Sometimes it's shameful. Sometimes it's painful. Whatever. I don't have time to even apply a feeling to it. It's just a fact.

I love prescription medications. Even just *having* the prescription makes me feel taken care of, like someone is watching out for me. But I'm not going down that route this time. I am going to take care of me for once. I am in charge and I will heal.

I've never actually been addicted to a prescription drug, but the tendency is there. I can feel it. I know that if someone prescribes an anti-psychotic or anti-depressant or anti-whatever, I will never be able to stop for fear that it will come back.

Sleep pills are like PEZ candy to me. A doctor suggested I take half a pill before bedtime to help with nausea when I was two months pregnant. I took more and more and now I'm up to two pills every night.

Wait, if I'm being honest, I'm up to three sleeping pills a night. Seriously, I almost lied to myself in my own journal. What is wrong with me?

Here's the test: If I can kick the shit out of whatever this is without medication, then I'm not schizophrenic. If I sink further and further into a crazy pool, then I'm schizophrenic.

August 7, 2001

I want to go back to the way I used to be. I used to be funny and fun. I used to worry about small stuff like a stupid sinus infection or getting in late to work.

Those worries truly were a waste a time, just like Dad said they were. My current worries truly are worry-worthy. This is survival.

I still panic, thinking that man is following me. I can control whether or not I kill myself, but I can't control if he attacks me and takes my daughter away from me. He still has that fucking picture of Parker and me. I hate it. I snap my head around when I feel this man, this horrible kidnapper, behind me. Ready to strike.

Sometimes I feel like he's in my house. I think he wants to strangle me and I have no idea how I would fight back if someone attacks me from behind. I'm not a strong person. Everyone knows that. I ask Derek to check the

Un-Perfect

basement to make sure no one is there. He said, "What do you mean 'to make sure no one is there'? You think someone is just hanging out in the corner of our basement eating our leftovers in the trash? What are you talking about?" I explained that it's possible. Maybe an ex-convict is hiding out in our basement and is planning to kill us. Derek laughed – what a funny joke. "Right, hahaha, maybe I should bring him a blanket and pillow. A nightlight in case he gets scared of the dark. Hahaha." It's not a joke. I'm serious, but I can't tell him that, so I laughed along with him.

I'm still recycling out the crappy, heart-banging images. It's exhausting and I probably look catatonic while I do it, but it has to be done. It gets me through the day and helps me feel like I have some control over this.

While the recycling gig is good, I need something to prevent me from killing myself. Every day I say, "Not today", but it is coming. I can feel it. There will be a day when I'm not afraid to jump from twenty stories up. I stare at the Foshay building every day from my office window.

My friends at work came rushing into my office last week, laughing hysterically, yelling, "Oh my God! Kelly, check this out. Grab the binoculars and look at the Foshay roof! You are going to DIE when you see this! I'm SERIOUS!"

People were having sex on the roof of the Foshay. On lunch break. Who goes back to work after that? Gross. But while it's totally humiliating, I envied those people for being on the roof and not considering a swift jump. They weren't thinking about dying, they were thinking about orgasms. To be such a free thinker!

My friends look at the Foshay building and just see a building… or two people having sex, which at least provides entertainment. It's just a building to them and they think nothing of it.

Want to know what I heard from that conversation? Two things:

I am going to DIE.

People are allowed to walk on the roof.

I could bring wire cutters to escape through the stupid wire fence that prevents people like me from jumping. It would be simple. I'm sure my friends had no intention of planting a suicide idea in my head, but that's what happened.

So yes, I could do it. I could jump from the Foshay building. Big deal. Everyone has that choice every single day. But fuck that. I'm living. I choose to live.

And I'm not looking back.

Instead of thinking about the suicide thought, I went shopping with my friends and bought some new shoes. Because if I'm going to be here, I deserve cute shoes. People who want to die don't invest in things like that because they won't need them. I, however, plan on living, which means I have a need for shoes.

So there. I have new shoes.

August 8, 2001

Since that sex-on-the-Foshay incident planted a suicide idea in my head, I realized I needed an "Anti-Suicide Campaign".

My campaign consists of Recycling Of the Mind and now daily notes to myself. It sounds egotistical, but for God's

Un-Perfect

sake, I have to force myself to remember why I need to live.

I started writing down five things for which I'm grateful. Every morning. A little love note to myself.

That sounds so stupid, but whatever.

Today's list:

1. I like to laugh.

2. I want to be Parker's mom. No one else can have that job.

3. Music.

4. My worn-out GAP jeans.

5. Trees/leaves rustling in the wind.

I've only been doing this for a couple days, but it feels good. All day I put my hands in my pockets and feel the piece of paper. It's usually dog-eared and soft by the end of the day because I rub the corners all day long.

I never have to pull it out because I know what's written on it and it keeps me alive. I throw it away at the end of the day. I hope Derek doesn't find them in the trash. I'm afraid he'll think I'm weird.

Anyway, the magic seems to be good only from morning to night.

For that day and that day only, I exist.

So far it's working. I'm still here. I'm not going

anywhere.

August 9, 2001 3:00 A.M.

Postpartum psychosis, or whatever I have, is not all terror-filled, horrific thoughts. I feel normal except for my psychotic whiplashes and thoughts of having a split personality.

The suicidal thinking was more intellectual, so I don't really count that as abnormal behavior. It was a back-up plan if my recovery route didn't work. But it will work because I'm tenacious when I focus my energy on things.

Sometimes, and this is incredibly rare, I think about the future.

I tentatively dare to think about growing old and having grandchildren. I close my eyes and I see Derek and me old and gray, playing with grandchildren.

As soon as my heart stretches out to embrace it, it moves further away, out of reach. Of course that future is not for me. I can barely make it through a day.

Since when did I receive a permission slip for the audacity to dream?

Hello. Welcome to the asylum of my head. Back and forth I go. Good

Un-Perfect

to bad. Bad to good.

But lately my mind dialogue is different. It's starting to happen in words again instead of images. That's new and I like it because it's less scary.

The bottom line is this: I still have gory images that would make a psychiatrist scream, but sometimes instead of just seeing images, I'm thinking in words, like normal people. I'm capable of having normal inner dialogue. Words hurt less than images. I don't know if this is due to my Recycling Of The Mind and my notes of gratitude, but whatever it is, I'm thankful for it.

Everyone is still here. Safe, healthy and happy. Just what I wished for.

The nightmares are so awful though. God, they just blow ass. I hate them. I hate them.

Last night I dreamed I was being chased and someone wanted to kill me. I ran and ran and ran, then got pissed and stopped running. I kicked the living shit out of a man in this nightmare. I didn't stop beating him even after he was dead. Maybe he was a metaphor for whatever I'm beating? That could be kind of cool if it's true. Maybe it's not about beating a real person, but rather beating whatever mental condition is threatening my life?

But then in the dream I got scared because I didn't know how to hide the body and everyone would find out that I'm a horrible, angry person. Hmmmm... I'm petrified of anyone finding out about what I have so I hide the "body" or rather, my mental madness. It scares me to think anyone could find out about this and label me a horrible person, so I hide how I'm feeling.

Maybe nightmares aren't so scary after all.

August 9, 2001

Oh for God's sake, I'm trying so hard not to kill myself and then I have Derek fighting me on bedtime. What is it with him and the lack of a bedtime routine? This is the only decision I can make. Why is he fighting me on it?

I'll announce at 8:30, "Okay, it's time for bed now." And he literally doesn't move his ass. Either that, or he'll start wrestling with Parker. What is that? We all sit peacefully watching TV or playing tea party and then as soon as I mention bedtime, he starts acting like a five-year-old.

Tonight he turned into a fire-breathing dragon and pretended to maul her and chased her around the house. I'm not a child psychologist, but something tells me that's not the calming routine needed to get a one-year-old into bed without a screaming match.

Little does he know I'm trying to crawl my way back to life and the life he's creating for me is not appealing.

I asked him why he doesn't do the fire-breathing dragon shit at 6:30. He looked at Parker and said, "Uh oh, Mommy's crabby."

No, Mommy's not crabby. Mommy just doesn't want to have sex with a fire-breathing dragon at midnight since she has to wake up at 6:00 a.m. for work.

Un-Perfect

Derek

8/9/01

I already have a mother. I don't think Kelly knows that because she tells me when it's time for bed. At 8:30 p.m. I'm a grown-up now, so I'm pretty confident I can figure out when I'm tired.

And you know what? If I want to be a dragon and make Parker laugh, that's my choice. I work until 7:00 p.m. some nights and I deserve to have more than ninety minutes with my kid.

That's it. This conversation is over. Parker can go to bed at 9:30 p.m. on the nights I work late. The world won't stop spinning if she goes to bed one hour later than what Kelly deems right.

Give me a break. She thinks she knows everything.

Note: Sometimes I wrestle with Parks at bedtime to prove to Kelly that she doesn't have ALL the control in the house. I can mess with the routine all I want. It's my life too.

August 9, 2001 AGAIN.

Okay, here's the deal on what I'm thinking: I am causing my own terror. But why would anyone choose to cause their own terror? Doesn't life serve up enough shit just on its own? Why would I choose to add a sprinkle of terror on top of my life?

I need to figure this out. My own head is making these thoughts, but I'm not in charge of them. Who took the wheel when I was on coffee break? I don't recall giving up the driver's seat. I don't understand why I can't control my own thinking.

But who am I now? How can I be witnessing, and realizing, and writing, about this awareness, but also doing the damage at the same time? Again, my only explanation is a split personality. I'm two people: One is thinking the thoughts and one is aware of the thoughts I'm thinking.

I feel like a dog chasing its tail. Around and around I go and I'll never catch it. Everything to understand is so frustratingly elusive, always floating just out of my reach.

Maybe I don't have postpartum stuff at all. I mean, it's been fifteen months since having Parker. Is that still considered postpartum? Maybe I'm just discovering that I have a split personality. How else can I explain the two lines of thought? One does the thinking and the other is aware of the thinking.

But I checked the definition of split personality and it says, "one personality is always dominant and not aware of the other." That is not the case for me. My lines of thought intersect and fight it out together. Unfortunately, I'm incredibly aware of each and every thought I produce.

I would probably welcome a split personality disorder. At least I could lose time and sink into beautiful oblivion, not remembering the blood-soaked remnants of my thinking.

Okay. So, since I'm aware of each and every thought and I don't black

Un-Perfect

out, I do not have a split personality. This leaves me with postpartum shit. Now what?

August 10, 2001 Lunch break

I brought my journal to work with me, and now I'm having an anxiety attack. What if I leave it somewhere and someone reads it? I really WILL have to jump off the Foshay if that happens.

But I need this journal, I need to get it out of my head and onto paper, otherwise it just bangs around in my ribcage.

I was writing in it and someone stopped by my desk and said, "Whatcha doin?" I'm wondering if she saw anything I wrote. What if she saw the words "die" or "terror" on one of the pages? I can't imagine the humiliation. I've got to stop thinking about that or it will drive me crazy.

Or in my case, crazier.

On my way to work this morning a psychic was on the radio station. Someone called in because they were afraid their loved one was addicted to drugs. The psychic sent out "gold swirls" around the addicted person and filled him with gold light. Since I'm addicted to my gory thoughts, I think I'll give this "gold swirl" stuff a try.

But a psychic? This guy sounded seriously nuts. But honestly, I don't give a shit if this sounds wacky because I AM wacky.

The nights are my black hole, so I need something to help me through the black. I usually find myself in the bathroom with an anxiety attack or crying. In the past, I thought of taking the blade out of my razor and ending the thoughts by ending me.

But I've decided I'm not going to kill myself over this stupid shit.

Recovery is not always a straight trajectory into the clouds. There are steps back. I expected this. Since I'm doing this without medication, I'm at risk because of my human capacity to recover.

That means I climb and slide like Parker's game of Chutes & Ladders. It's all me and it's the way I want it. I want to be aware and feel when I slide. Last night was a slide. I'm okay with it and actually, I'm proud that I didn't consider suicide. Baby steps.

But the night is so dark, it feels suffocating. There is nothing to distract me from my unworldly, unholy, thoughts.

I usually try to postpone going to sleep by going through a strict bedtime routine. I close the door only 75% of the way. If it's too open, I can't sleep because it feels like anything can come in. But if it's closed all the way, I can't breathe.

The curtains have to be completely closed together so the moonlight doesn't come in at all. If shards of light slice through a crack in the curtains, I

Un-Perfect

can't sleep and I'm afraid the morning light will wake me up too early and I won't get seven hours of sleep.

Sometimes the vent ticks when the air conditioner kicks on, so I wear ear plugs. I can still hear the ticking through the ear plugs and it drives me crazy. *Tick.* Then I count: One, two, three, four, five six. *Tick.* One, two, three, four, five, six, seven, eight *(where is it?)* nine, ten, elev-*Tick.* One, two, three, *Tick-tick. Oh, now it's double ticks? What the fuck?* There is no rhythm to the ticking and I hate that. It should be every certain amount of seconds, nice and even, but it's not and that drives me insane.

If a tiny light is left on from the DVD player, I have to cover it up with a post-it note because if I wake up in the middle of the night and see a red "eye" staring back at me, I will think the eye of Satan is staring at me. I even hate the red light on the smoke alarm, but it's too high on the ceiling. I can't reach it to put a post-it note on it and Derek will think I'm crazy if I get the ladder to crawl up there to put a post-it note on a light.

Anyway, last night I sat in the bathroom, wrapping my arms around me, the only hug I could find. I stared at the floor thinking about medication vs. no medication. While my choice is no medication, I don't care if one woman takes meds and another doesn't. Frankly, I don't have the energy to be worrying about what anyone else is doing. I have to be selfish right now.

If someone is killing their kids or jumping from buildings, I have to look away. It's not right, but I don't have a choice. It's not going to help this world if I jump with them.

Every night is a slippery slope into The Crazy Pool. I don't know what else to call it. I don't know what I'm dealing with. It's like getting into the boxing ring and fighting a ghost.

Swirling gold streamers.

Why not? Why can't I have gold streamers? I sat at my desk and imagined gold party streamers swirling inside of me, making me bright. I imagined them pushing black, evil energy out through the bottom of my feet. Like black powder. Poof! Gone. I prayed to God, or whatever Divine Dog is the source of all life, and I told myself that I am good. Over and over again. I let my heart communicate this message: "Please fill me with pure gold. Make me good again. I am good." Goddammit, I *am* good. Right?

That felt kind of cool. Well, now back to work.

August 10, 2001 night

I'm working so hard at filtering incoming information that I cannot allow anything into my head unless it has a good vibe. This means no news, no disturbing movies, no disturbing TV shows, and not listening to other people's tragedies. Some of the previews on TV scare the crap out of me.

After my gold swirling, a colleague came to my desk and started telling me about a woman that died and I stopped her mid-sentence and said, "No, no, you have to stop. I'm totally serious. I will diagnose myself with whatever she had and have my death certificate written before you're done with the story. No way. I can't listen to this." I think I literally shooed her away with my hand like she was a fly. I didn't mean to be rude about it. I feel bad that I did that.

She walked away looking over her shoulder, shaking

Un-Perfect

her head back and forth like I was nuts. She has no idea. I hope I didn't hurt her feelings, but I have to censor everything around me if I'm going pull myself out of this hellhole.

But it's so annoying. Why do people love a tragic story? Is it because they need assurance that it won't happen to them? Everyone knows a person like this. They're like ambulance chasers and emotional dependency is their payoff. I see it as a narcissistic desire to be the center of everyone's life.

To these people I say, "If I want you to have a front row seat in my life, I will invite you to take a seat. Otherwise, please be quiet. I'm trying not to kill myself today and you're making it almost impossible."

DEREK

8/10/01

"I only got six hours of sleep last night."

This is Kelly's Daily Sleep Report.

So? I did too, but we all need to move on with the day. Parents of small children don't get a lot of sleep, but she seems to think that she's entitled to seven hours of sleep. Otherwise she just seems out of it.

The daily sleep reports are getting old. I get it.

We go to bed at the same time and wake up together. I get the same amount of sleep as she does and if I get four hours, then I get four hours. I'm not going to bitch about it all day.

Then she'll nap to make up the difference. I don't think I've ever taken a nap, but for some reason, she gets to take them.

Note: "What if that happens to Parker?" This is what Kelly asks me about a million times a week. Am I supposed to know the answer to that question? Because I don't.

August 11, 2001

I'm healing, I know I'm healing, but I'm still sick. With what, I have no idea. I don't understand what has been happening to me and that is scary.

Maybe I truly am mentally ill and no one has caught it. I think it's a postpartum thing. I don't know why I'm experiencing it after she's one, but I still think it's a postpartum gig.

I hate not understanding what is ruining my life. I'm dealing with what feels like "bad air." I can't touch it, define it, grab it, or fix it. It sucks. I have no control. None.

Un-Perfect

I still worry when I sleepwalk, wondering where I've been. I still have repulsive images of people dying. And as much as I try to police incoming information, I come across a headline with a tragic story and my heart rolls out the welcome mat. I take the world's tragedy on as my own.

I went to get my eyes checked last week and there was a little girl, about eight-years-old, sitting next to me. Her head was wrapped in bandages and I immediately wanted to start crying because whatever happened to her should not have happened. She's a sweet little girl. And her dad was sitting with her, gently touching her shoulders, and kissing her bandages. I could feel his pain and soaked it into my soul.

I was called into my examination room, where I had to wait another twenty minutes. There's a reason I'm called a patient when I'm at a doctor's office. Because that's what is required of me: Patience. Anyway, I heard the nurses talking outside my door, obviously not aware that I could hear them. They were explaining the severity of the girl's terminal cancer. I still break down and cry when I think about that beautiful, sweet girl.

Derek said, "But it's not Parker."

But it *could* be.

And to think there is a mother out there with a dying child is just too much for me. It's like I don't have a filter on my heart like everyone else. Pain, sorrow, anguish, and tragedy seem to cuddle up inside of me. Everyone else reads the paper, watches the news, and goes to movies without any anxiety about what might get lodged in their hearts.

They digest disturbing information and then quickly release it with relief that it doesn't affect their lives. I don't have a release button. I literally live out every tragedy in my head. I'll focus on the exact steps taken, what people were feeling at each point, how it would feel physically, how it would feel emotionally and then I'll ruminate with the worst parts, playing those tidbits over and over again.

I need to take great care of myself and get rest. I sleepwalk when I'm overtired. I don't drink much at Happy Hour because I know I can't ever be out of control. Stumbling into the house drunk and waking up the next day would be too much, wondering if I destroyed anyone or anything while I was drunk. Whatever control I do have, cannot not be sacrificed by drinking a couple glasses of wine.

My bedtime routine is working fine. All I care about is getting at least seven hours of sleep. The door is three-fourths shut and moonlight is closed off. I sleep with an eye mask, ear plugs, and sleeping pills.

It's working and I'm sleeping sans nightmares, so I will continue with this route as long as it works. I've never been superstitious, but I am now. I used to open umbrellas inside the house and walk under ladders. I've broken mirrors. I've always done the opposite of what people thought was superstitious because I thought it was such bullshit. Now, I'm too afraid to test any superstitions.

August 12, 2001 Morning

I wake up at 6:00 a.m. to shower and if for some reason Parker decides to wake up early, I'm screwed. That's what happened today. There is no way I can get myself ready with a fifteen-month-old.

She was screaming in her booster seat because I had to run downstairs to iron my clothes and she was pissed because she couldn't see me. So while standing in my bra and

Un-Perfect

panties, I was singing (screaming), "You Are My Sunshine"
from the basement while frantically ironing my clothes.

She screamed, kicked and threw all her food on the
floor.

I blow-dried my hair while holding her on my hip,
but she hates the air in her face so she threw a tantrum and
knocked her fist against my jaw. That counts as a punch to
the face.

I yelled, "God! You just HIT me! What do you
WANT!? Here, eat the Cheerios. Put them in your face
and eat them!"

And of course she's overtired because Derek decided to wrestle with her until 9:30 p.m. last night. She was up at 5:30 a.m. all piss and vinegar. I don't blame her. But I do blame *him*. He has no idea what I have to do in the morning.

I have to catch a bus to the city by 8:35 or I'm late to work. I have to feed her breakfast and change her clothes because she's a sloppy eater, I have to make sure she wears tennis shoes instead of the sparkly sandals which invites a tantrum. "No! Don't want those!" I just cram them on her feet and scoop her up to go. I can't reason with a toddler. I've tried it. It doesn't work. Then as I drop her off at Peggy's, she grabs my neck and cries because she doesn't want me to leave. This breaks my heart because she finally likes me and now I'm leaving her. So I cry on the way to the bus stop and wipe my tears away before anyone sees me fall apart.

I desperately want to stay home with her so we can finally enjoy each

Kelly Nordstrom

other, but I have to work because we have bills to pay. I hate it, but I can't tell Derek because he will just feel guilty for not making enough money. I don't want to make him feel bad. He's a great husband and father. But it hurts my heart every morning to leave her – she's available to me all day, yet I choose to go to work instead. The guilt is unbearable. We could sell the house and move into a cheap townhome and I could drive a used car instead of a new one. We could make changes so I could stay home, but I don't want Derek to resent me.

Anyway, by the time I get to work I've been spit on, punched, kicked, heart broken, and screamed at. Nice. Then I go to work for more of the same. No I wonder I was suicidal.

August 12, 2001

I didn't realize it, but when I do my nighttime "Gold Swirling", it's considered meditating. How weird is that? Washing out all the dark powder with gold streamers is meditating. I would have never guessed I could meditate.

But here I am, meditating every night and I read that it's good for the soul. It has the ability to rope in the sun, moon, and stars like a celestial cowgirl and manifest all our hopes and dreams. I like this idea of having my own power and tapping into a Source that has a never ending reserve.

I need that. It makes whatever I'm experiencing seem so small. I have the power to turn this around. I'm already doing it. I believe in the power of myself.

Un-Perfect

Images are getting less frequent. I know this because I'm listening to what people are saying and I see only them while they're speaking. It's a beautiful thing. I'm connecting with people again.

I'm one of them again. Connected with the Whole again.

My Notes Of Five Today:
1. *I have gold swirls protecting me.*
2. *Parker's hugs.*
3. *Derek's laugh.*
4. *I have good friends.*
5. *I am positively powerful.*

And I'm laughing, truly LAUGHING, when I find something funny. Not because the old Kelly would have laughed, but because I think something is funny and I can't prevent the laugh from bubbling up and out.

So this is working for me... getting rest, censoring what I watch/read/hear, meditating, Notes of Five and Recycling Of The Mind.

I have tenacious hope that I am pulling myself out of this hole. I WILL be better. That's a fact.

I'm on my way to a better me. I'm not even going back to who I used to be, I'm evolving into something better. Take THAT, you motherfucking disease.

August 13, 2001

I'm thinking about medication again today and why I don't just bite the bullet and go on it. But I don't even know what I have, so how can I trust that someone outside of my experience will know? What if I'm a schizo and they think I'm depressed? What if I have a split personality and they say I have postpartum psychosis?

It scares the hell out of me that someone could get it wrong and put me on the wrong medication. Oh my God, that would throw me off the ledge.

But if someone did get it right and I went on the right medication, I wouldn't have to rally in my bathroom in the middle of the night anymore. I wouldn't worry about being Satan's daughter and being schizophrenic. I would sleep without having to go through a nighttime routine. I wouldn't have to meditate all the time. I wouldn't have to carry around five reasons not to kill myself. Good Lord, that sounds pitiful.

Yes, my tiny human mortal body can become defective and medication can reset the wiring. But I also think a lot of my suffering is a symptom of all the "soul shredding" I'm doing on the inside. All those ticker tapes I play across my brain, accusing myself of not being good enough, not smart enough, not pretty enough, not perfect enough, not successful enough. How can I stop that ticker tape? I think medication can fix that. But I think I can fix it too. I mean, I think I AM fixing it. I think I'm getting better.

Why can't I have a strategy with offense and defense like football? I

Un-Perfect

need a strong offensive line to prevent postpartum shit from happening and a mean defensive line to battle back if it tries seeping back in. Where's my fucking team? Who's got my back? I'm a quarterback without a team.

I mean, look how many people are involved in a meaningless game with men in tights, yet there is nothing out there for a woman that just birthed a human being? Give me a break. A quarterback has personal trainers, coaches, nutritionists, and his entire team of peers. He is surrounded by support. I'm alone.

How fucked up is our society that we care more about men running up and down a field with a football than we do about a woman learning how to raise a child in this world? For God's sake, if it means anything, my baby could be a future season ticket-holder if I don't slip through the cracks.

August 13, 2001 Bedtime

I was in the zone today. All Zen and cool and calm. And then bedtime. I announced that it's time for Parker to go to bed and Derek just sat there with her on his lap, not moving a muscle.

I said, "Hello? Do you not hear me or do you just choose not to respond? Can I at least get a head nod or something so I know you're not losing your hearing?"

I was so frustrated that I kissed her on the head and said, "Daddy's going to put you to bed tonight. Love you!" I went into the bedroom and read my book. And then prayed it would be a rough bedtime -that she would kick and scream and punch him in the face like she does with me in the mornings.

Instead he got lucky. It was peaceful and easy. He got into bed and I said, "Oh I bet you just feel like Parent Of The Year now, yeah? Maybe you should do bedtime every night since I do every morning alone." Seems only fair to me.

But underneath all the anger I realized maybe I'm the one making bedtime all stressed out and noisy. I would never admit it to Derek, but I think I'm the one that needs to make some changes. And maybe he does too, but honestly, his journey is his own business. Not mine.

DEREK

8/13/01

I have only one thing to say and I'm going to take up an entire page to say it:

Can someone tell my wife to calm the hell down when it comes to bedtime?

Un-Perfect

August 14, 2001

No more secrets. I've got to take the chance that Derek may not like me if he knows what's been going on. I can't sit here and worry about accidentally "outing" my secret.

I sat him down and told him about my postpartum stuff. It feels a little overly dramatic because a doctor never diagnosed me with anything. It's one thing simply carrying this knowledge inside of me, but trying to explain to another person without that stamp of validation from a doctor feels less "official". More like being a whiny baby that wants attention.

I told him that when Parker was an infant, I kept thinking icky, weird thoughts, but couldn't help it. I explained that I *think* I was depressed and I *think* I had postpartum psychosis, but not sure.

This is why it doesn't feel real; I still don't know what was, or still is, wrong with me. What if I'm schizophrenic and I'm labeling it a postpartum thing? I'm baffled and it's frustrating to not understand it.

I told him about the day at the beach and that I worried I could have killed her because I wasn't confident that my ten fingers could keep her alive. We didn't go into any more detail because he was freaked out. He just froze and looked around at the walls wondering where this was coming from, as if answers were hiding around the corner. No way was I going to tell him I thought I was Satan's daughter. No way.

He raked his fingers through his hair like he always does when he's overwhelmed and said, "You need to tell me if you ever have these thoughts again." He promised to get me help if it happens again.

His reaction after learning only a sprinkle of the truth makes me realize how dire my situation actually was (and still is, to a degree). Again, it's one thing to toss it around in your own head, but to release it into the world and have someone validate it is something else. It becomes real.

The words I speak seem to crystallize in the air and become touchable and solid. To have someone else look at them from the outside feels even more shameful and embarrassing. Derek is seeing the facts without the noise of my mind trying to resist it.

When I first began thinking that I may have had (still have to some extent) postpartum psychosis, I told myself things like, "This is only temporary and you can handle it. Today you've had good thoughts too…"

But Derek is hearing the jagged raw facts and they're just sitting there in the open without any care or softness added to them. It's like throwing sharp rocks at his heart. They hurt more without the cushion of desensitization. I slowly walked into this stuff, one rock at a time. But for Derek, I tossed an armful at him without thinking it would surprise, shock or hurt him. The sad thing is I have about a hundred more rocks to put on the table. But not now.

He beat himself up for not seeing through my charade. "What husband doesn't see that his wife was hurting? Why didn't you say anything?" I explained that I thought he would leave me and take Parker.

He said he would never leave me when I was hurting, but if I needed help and it required a hospital stay, he would push for it. Fair enough. If I was having thoughts of harming our child, he wanted me to be in a place where everyone was safe until I was better. I don't know that he understands that thoughts of harming our child was based on the FEAR of her being harmed, not that I WANTED to harm her. There's a big difference. I tried explaining this to him, but I don't think he understands the difference.

Hearing this makes me afraid of myself, like he's talking about another

Un-Perfect

person.

But it feels good to untie the knot and let my secret drain out, even if I didn't explain every rancid detail or how I was cloaked in heavy despair.

I didn't talk about how scared I was. I didn't explain that I sat in the bathroom more than once trying to convince myself that I was okay. I didn't tell him that I considered removing the blades from my pink razor and slitting my wrists. There's a lot of shame still stuck in there, clinging to my ribs, preventing me from coming totally clean with it all. But it's a start.

And isn't that the case with any secret? You spoon-feed the information to your loved one, gauging the reaction, letting it digest, then a few more spoonfuls, until most of it is out of you and into your spouse. When we release secrets, we are lifting heavy stones from our own hearts and inserting them into another person. It is a delicate process.

And let's face it, this is the first time I have ever said these words out loud. They are clunky and coated in embarrassment and shame, making each word uncomfortable to release. I could only get out a few sentences before it clogged up in my throat.

He stared at me the rest of the night as if he was waiting for me to mutate into a serial killer.

We were lying on the sofa together and he said, "How do you feel now? Do you feel good? How do I know if you're faking?" How *will* he know if I'm faking happiness? That's a fair question.

I have to learn how to show my vulnerability and fear. I honestly don't understand how to do that without feeling like a wimp, but I will try.

DEREK

8/14/01

SHOCKED.

I'M SHOCKED.

It's not every day that your wife confesses to almost drowning your daughter at the beach. No one is ever prepared to hear that coming from their spouse's mouth. How does a person hate what they are thinking, but they think it anyway? That makes no fucking sense to me.

I feel like I'm on Defcon-5, military watch to see any slight change in her. I've been awake all night to make sure she doesn't sleepwalk.

She says she's fine, but what if she's faking it? This is not like faking an orgasm, this is faking life. What she told me is not the Kelly I know. The Kelly I know doesn't crumble. She's steady and unshakeable.

If this could happen to her, it can happen to anyone. She's the most unlikely target. Always happy, always positive, always supportive. Why would those things add up to, what is it called? Oh yeah...postpartum psychic or psychotic?

No, no. Psychosis. That's what she said.

I have no idea what postpartum psychosis means.

Un-Perfect

Didn't the woman that drowned her kids have that? This is not good. I don't get it. I don't get how a person hates a thought but thinks about it anyway. I don't FUCKING GET IT. It sounds ridiculous. If you don't like what you're thinking, then don't think it. It's that simple.

I didn't even know there was a psychosis thing. I thought there was only a postpartum depression thing and I would be able to detect it if Kelly was lying in bed in all day, moping around the house. That's what I was looking for. So since Kelly still had a smile on her face, I thought we escaped all this shit.

Goddamn it, how does a person have a thought and know it doesn't make sense, but can't stop thinking it anyway? HOW? Someone needs to explain this to me, because Kelly can't.

I don't mean to be an asshole about this, but I'm a little scared. I mean, did she ever have thoughts of killing me? At least I could fight her off, but my baby? I want to have Parker sleeping in our bed next to me now every night to make sure she stays safe.

I've trusted Kelly with my life for eleven years now and never once did my trust in her crumble, but I have to say it's a little tested. I don't know if I'm sounding like a dick or not, I'm just trying to process this.

> Forget cheaters and their affairs.
> My wife almost killed our daughter, and there is simply no part of my brain that understands how to compute that.

If she says it's over, then it's over. That's it then. I have to trust that she's going to tell me if she starts feeling that feeling again, whatever it is, exactly. I don't know. I don't know what to do.

And what's worse is that if I did see that she was suffering from this psychosis shit, I wouldn't have a clue how to help her.

She said she would have to go to the hospital, but where in the hospital? Is there a certain wing or area for this that I should know about? I don't get it. Do I drive to the ER? Isn't there a number I should call or something?

This is freaking me out, I'm not built for this shit.

Note: What kind of husband doesn't know his wife is going crazy? She didn't seem nuts, so how would I have known?

> *How did I NOT know?*

> *I don't know my own wife. I feel betrayed. I hate that she kept a secret from me.*

Un-Perfect

I'm sorry. I'm so sorry.

I'm sorry I didn't see it. I'm sorry I wasn't there when she needed me. I'm sorry she was hurting. I'm sorry I don't know how to handle it. I'm just so fucking sorry that I don't get how a person doesn't want to think something but thinks it anyway. That really IS crazy to me.

August 15, 2001

Derek doesn't understand that I'm still IN IT. I don't want him to worry about me. And I DEFINITELY don't want Parker sleeping in our bed with us because for one, it makes me feel like a monster and two, I've worked so hard to get her to sleep in her own room. I need sleep to pull out of this.

My nighttime structure is still very stringent. Derek tries talking to me while we're lying in bed, but I have to take out my ear plugs, un-strap my face mask, and remove my mouth guard (my dentist explained that I'm a teeth grinder, which did not come as a surprise to me).

By the time I'm ready to listen he says, "Forget it. I love you." Then I have to re-plug, re-strap and re-insert.

I should just wear a helmet to bed.

Kelly Nordstrom

Parker still wakes up sometimes and that throws me into a tizzy. I try and go back to sleep, but wonder if I suffocated her, then go back in to check her breathing, then wonder if I suffocated her that time, then go back in... I will do that for an hour or two until I finally wake Derek and ask him to check on her. That's another reason she can't sleep with us. Derek thinks she'll be safer. I worry I could roll over and accidentally suffocate her.

For some reason, getting out of bed in the middle of the night sends me into this vicious cycle that I can't seem to stop. I try meditating, but I can't concentrate until I know she's okay. Thankfully, she doesn't get up too often.

It's the last piece of the puzzle - but it's not responding to my tools. It's still here. I know that it is not rational to think I suffocated her. I know I would never harm her. I remind myself that it is not real, but it still sticks no matter what I do. I worry about every single thing or person in this world that could harm her. My protection is on overdrive. Unfortunately, I am a person that COULD harm her. I never would, but I could. For some reason, every person in this world could harm her... except Derek. I don't believe he could. To me, he's the one person in this world that does not threaten harm in any way to either Parker or myself. So I need to have Derek check on her before I can go to sleep. I never believe she's okay until he confirms that she's okay.

Lack of sleep does not send him spiraling into weird shit, but it does for me, so he's quickly becoming the nighttime caretaker. But he doesn't know why. He doesn't know I have this nighttime worry. He just thinks I used to worry about her being harmed when she was an infant.

While he knows part of my secret, he does not understand that it is still going on. I positioned it as a thing that happened to me when she was born. I don't know why I lied. I guess because his reaction was so severe, I couldn't possibly choke out the words, "I'm still in it and working hard to get out of it."

Even now, with him thinking it was something in the past, he looks at

Un-Perfect

me like he doesn't know me. He watches me with Parker now, which makes me feel like a convict that was just released from jail.

This is why I didn't go all the way with the truth. I can't stand these looks of fear, wondering what I'm capable of. There is some lost trust between us now. He used to be able to depend on me and count on me, but I can tell that's gone. I have a lot of work ahead of me if I want to regain that trust.

We don't talk about it. It's almost as if the conversation didn't even happen. He doesn't want to think I'm crazy and I don't want to remember that I was (or still am).

Nightmares are still hanging around which bug the hell out of me. Last night I dreamed that I pushed this spiky dresser up a ramp next to our bed. Then after all that work I realized if I let it go, it would fall back down the ramp and into our bed and kill Derek and me.

So I let the spiky dresser go then ran for the light and turned it on. Really, in real life, I tried to beat the spiky dresser from hitting our bed by racing to the light. I turned on the light and Derek yelled, "What are you doing?! God!" So it was fine. Still alive.

August 15, 2001 Bedtime

I hit the gym today for the first time in forever. I read somewhere that "Sauna therapy" is supposed to be good for helping with depression, so I drove to the club after work today.

A few older ladies around seventy joined me in my "sweat bath" and we had a good conversation. I was telling them that sauna therapy is a real thing; it's been known to relieve depression, lower blood pressure, and sweat the fat off our asses.

And then I got a glimpse of one of those asses up close and personal. My new friend Mildred took off her towel and lotioned her body next to me. As she bent over to lubricate her ankles, I could have reached out and slapped her ass. Good Lord.

Mildred left after her naked body was hydrated. I was alone again trying to meditate with my gold swirls and spin the image of her ass out of my mind when another guest arrived.

With a thong in her hands.

I must have looked shocked or maybe even said out loud - *What the fuck are you going to do with that thong?* - Because she immediately started explaining herself. "I'm so sorry, but this is the only underwear I have today, so I washed them in the sink and now they need to dry out."

I was staring at fabric that was, up until ten minutes earlier, in someone's butt crack.

She gently laid her wet thong out next to the coals on the wooden frame and left to get dressed and blow-dry her hair. I was held hostage to staring at it for the rest of my sauna therapy. It took about 1.5 seconds to realize this wasn't going to work.

But you know what? On the drive home I laughed out loud to myself. Life has funny things in it. Have funny things always been around me and I just forgot to look around and see them?

Un-Perfect

August 16, 2001

With each sweet moment, I want the clock to hold still for just a moment, freeze everything so I can brand it onto my brain. All these memories are so fleeting, it's like trying to catch fireflies in a jar so I can hold them and look at them from all angles.

I want to take the time to appreciate each and every one of them. But I can't. Time just keeps moving forward, more fireflies to catch, never enough time to catch them.

Parker could grab my cheeks and kiss me and then skip off in her dress giggling before I even realized what happened. I'm desperate to remember that her hands smelled of strawberry jelly when she grabbed my cheeks. I want to remember how her hair blew in the wind, blonde ringlets dancing in the air when she skipped away.

And then the wind stops and my cheek grows cold. Poof! In the blink of an eye, it's now a memory.

The ticking of the clock always marks the passing of something. *Tick*, gone, *tick*, gone, *tick*, gone. Even as a kid I remember thinking, "There it goes again! This exact moment in this exact time will never happen again. There it goes *again*! Gone, and I can never make it happen again."

Sometimes I'd just stand in front of my parent's grandfather clock and watch it tick away, aware that everything that was happening around me was never going to happen again. *Tick.* My sister Kim would never grab her tennis racket and push her feathered hair off her forehead while she walked out the front door. *Tock*. My Dad would never sing, "Blue Eyes" in that exact tone, while pouring a glass of milk. *Tick*. My mom would never cut material with orange flowers on it in that exact way again. *Tock*. Kari would never be huddled in the corner in our hanging bamboo chair whispering to her boyfriend with her knees folded in her chest.

I remember thinking, "This is how I got to be ten years old already. With each tick that I'm watching now, I'm getting closer to eleven. It's moving too fast!"

All of that was happening while I watched a few seconds tick on the grandfather clock and it would never happen again. What was more terrifying to me was that my life was always happening that way, but I wasn't always aware of it.

Time is sneaky like that. It's like treading water at the beach and you look back to see you're a half mile from shore when you didn't even realize the waves were gently drawing you out the entire time. The trick is to appreciate where you are without missing the passing of it. Life moves like water.

I will only cause suffering if I'm grasping at each and every droplet that slides through my fingers. Life flows over sharp rocks sometimes and when we sign up for life, we sign up for everything. The rocks, the waterfalls, the peaceful flow.

I tried telling Derek about my new philosophy on life. It helps me to put my experience into perspective, whereas I think it scares the shit out of him. I'm guessing he doesn't want me to change; he just wants the old Kelly back. But I can't find her anywhere. I don't remember who that was before all of this happened.

We still don't talk about the postpartum stuff (of course I didn't mention that I was concerned that I was schizophrenic). I don't even know if

Un-Perfect

that's what I had or still have. There is no need to hash any details or ask if he's lost trust in me. I don't think I can handle the answer, so I don't ask.

8/17/01 Sunday Muffins at Mom's

We were hanging out at the counter this morning and I told my sisters and Mom that I think I had some postpartum stuff, "like the scary kind" as I described it. I mentioned how awful it was to chop up vegetables because knives could hurt Parker. And how I'd see her car seat tumble onto the freeway. I explained that it was really weird and scary.

They do not know I'm still in it. They do not know I thought (still think?) I'm Satan's daughter. They do not know I'm being stalked by a man that wants to kill me and steal Parker. They do not know that I might have a split personality. I don't mention the fact that I may be adopted because I can't bear to know if it's true.

Instead of a collective gasp, I got quiet compassion. This surprised me. They didn't ridicule me or judge me. "Oh Kelly, that must have been terrible to go through it alone. How are you feeling now?" I explained that I feel good, but I wanted them to know that I could be reaching out and if I do reach out, then I really need it.

The thing about me is that I don't ask for help until it's dire. Most people, I think, ask for help when they start feeling the stress of something. Me? I wait until I'm at the end of my rope and would probably call them from the ledge. "Hey, remember I mentioned that I'd call you if I needed some help? Well, I'm on the ledge of the Foshay Building downtown Minneapolis. I could really use you now if you're available. Is that cool? Are you too busy? If you're too busy, I could probably wait a while. It's not too windy today, so I should be fine."

So yes, I've got them set like second string linebackers in case I get hit again, but they can't help unless I tell them. I seem to only be able to talk about this as if it's in the past. I can't bring myself to say, "I'm still in it."

They, like Derek, are baffled I faked my way through it (still faking it). No one can understand how I hid it. They have no idea I'm still hiding it. If they only knew the monstrosity of the secret I still have tucked away. I cannot imagine what their reaction would be.

Un-Perfect

They didn't ridicule me. They didn't judge me.

Maybe this really *is* my family and I'm not adopted. I want so badly to know that I really am part of this family. I wish I could ask for a blood test, but I know they would think I'm nuts. I want to be special enough to share their DNA and all their good to be in my bones. Could I really have all that good stuff in me? Yeah, I think so.

August 17, 2001 Bedtime

I came across my scrapbook that I did when Parker was first born. I'm guessing that when I die (when I'm a 100, not now), she won't know what her mother looked like.

In fact, she may wonder if I attended graduations, plays, or even family trips. I never seem to make it into the pictures. I have no evidence to show that I was a part of this family because I'm cut off, cut out, or simply not photographed. Every picture is of Derek and Parker.

I feel like I'm always trying to smash Parker's face next to mine so I know that at least my nose will make it into the picture. We came across a home video recently with Parker playing underneath a toy and I actually maneuvered

Kelly Nordstrom

my body underneath it next to her body so there could be footage of me next to her.

You know what Derek did? He actually moved the camera off my face and focused the video camera onto plain carpet instead of me. So the video is Parker's head and about 3 feet of carpet.

What the hell is that about? I must have been too preoccupied to notice this crap until now.

There is a picture of Parker and me. She was in her Bjorn, *attached to my body*, and he still cut out my head. All of these pictures are filled with slices of me...a nose, a ponytail, an arm. I'm like a distorted mannequin that came along for the ride.

Does he not see me smiling and posing through the goddamn lens of the camera? I am a human being trying to capture a moment in time so when I'm 98, I have proof that I haven't always been a decaying bag of bones. I need to remember that indeed I had white teeth and bright eyes. I had energy and strength. I was a mother that played with her daughter.

But when I'm 98, I'm going to look at pictures that may or may not resemble my eyelid, nose, hand or collarbone. I'm sure it will be confusing to go through old family albums while I sit in the nursing home wondering, "Who the hell is that? The nanny? Did we even have a nanny?"

I showed Derek the book and reminded him of the video of Parker and carpet. He doesn't see the big deal. "I don't get it. Why do you need the picture? You're there. Why do you need a picture to remember the day?"

He thought I was being an egotistical snob that loves looking at herself.

Un-Perfect

I went into an exhausting tirade about how, as a mother, I need to remember how it felt to hold Parker's body next to mine. I need to see the glow on my face when I smelled the jelly on her lips. It goes by so fast. I need to document as much of it as possible so I can remember it. It's how I'm wired.

It's not about having a picture of *me*. It's about seeing me with my daughter and remembering the day and what we said and how little she sounds when I laugh with her. Maybe I feel the need to see pictures that document a good day for me after all the hell I'm going through.

It's not about the picture, it's about the experience and when I look at it I know that I felt good that day. I like having proof that I was here on this earth with my family. I exist. I love. I laugh.

I will see these pictures when I'm 98 and allow myself to sink back into the memory more clearly.

I still don't think he gets it. He thinks I'm a narcissist that loves looking at herself. Nice

DEREK

8/17/01

What is the big deal about pictures?

I'm not a photographer. I don't have a creative "eye" when I snap pictures of my family, so what? I thought Kelly was going to have a meltdown trying to explain the need for her to be in more pictures. It's all about her and I can't deliver. I get it. I didn't see the postpartum shit and now I'm a prick because I cut her out of pictures.

>   *Note: I can't do anything right.*

August 18, 2001

> *Derek only knows tiny fragments of my secret. But even knowing only bits of the secret, I feel like he sees me as fragile and vulnerable now. Someone that has cracked and could crack again.*
>
> *That is not who he married. He married someone that is dependable and solid. And now that's not who I am, so I'm afraid that he's reevaluating to whom he committed the rest of his life.*
>
> *We're only seven years into this marriage and I've already revamped my character. I wouldn't blame him if he served me with divorce papers. It would finally be the other shoe that dropped. Finally.*
>
> *I'm not the woman I said I was. I tried to be someone I'm not and I fooled him into marrying me.*

But I hope he likes me even after all this shit. I'm feeling incredibly vulnerable and naked, but I think it's good. Secrets have a way of rotting a marriage. It seethes just underneath the hugs and "I love you's". When he says "I love you", I want to know he loves all of me. Even the bad parts.

If I have a secret, it will always be tucked in the back of my head that he

Un-Perfect

doesn't quite love me all the way. I hope my husband loves me. The real me. The one that tripped and stumbled. The one that has to filter all the information she reads, sees, and hears.

If the tables were turned and he confessed that he was worried about harming our daughter, I would be afraid that he would still be capable of doing something terrible. It would be difficult to understand that he didn't WANT to harm her, he just worried that he COULD. How would I know if he really doesn't have those thoughts anymore? I would be watching him closely and asking him how he feels every minute of every day. "How's your breakfast honey? Feel like committing suicide or tossing around some knives today? Just curious. No? Oh good. Okay, then."

Seriously, how is a spouse to cope with this information? I didn't even mention that I was suicidal. He was so shocked after telling him about the beach, knives, and the car-seat-on-the-freeway images, I had to stop to protect his heart. It was breaking. I was so much worse than he can imagine. I can barely incorporate these thoughts into my *own* head. There's no way I can sink that enormity into his heart.

Sometimes I get glimpses of how strong I am, but most times I just see a breakable person in the mirror. It's hard to accept that piece into my identity because if I let that in, then who knows what else will break me? What else is out there with the capacity to send me back into a hole? I don't want to see myself as a frail little egg. I want to be a steel guardrail. Unshakeable. But I'm not. I shook. Somehow I have to see myself as someone that can be fragile. It's going to take some time to adjust how I see myself. Un-perfect is good.

I still don't understand what was, and to an extent, still is wrong with me. I don't know what I have or why. And in order to explain it to another person, I have to understand it myself before telling my full story.

August 19, 2001

Today is a "jelly-side down" day. Know what that is? It's when the day is so busy running, literally, from one thing to another that you don't have time to eat or pee.

I hadn't had a morsel of food until 7:00 p.m., so I made an English muffin with strawberry jelly. I was walking across the kitchen and dropped it. Jelly side down.

I yelled "MOTHERFUCKER! JELLY SIDE DOWN!"

I'm not proud of my reaction and apologized to Parker who, by the look on her face, was terrified. I pulled myself together and said, "Parker, I'm not proud of how I just handled this situation. Please do not say that bad word."

But the one "meal" I made for myself was now lying on the floor, jelly side down. I couldn't handle it. If it landed jelly side up, everything would have been fine. I would have picked it up and ate it. But I couldn't pick it up and eat it because I haven't washed the floors in at least three weeks.

I dream of being sent away to a resort where everything is white and talking is not permissible. Meditation is the only activity allowed. I imagine that my room does not have windows and no one cares if I emerge from the room or not. I could sleep for sixteen hours if I wanted to.

Un-Perfect

And then when I'm well-rested, a healthy dinner would be waiting for me.

And if an English muffin was served with this dinner, it would be jelly side up.

August 20, 2001 Morning

Music always speaks to me and my latest tune is Staind's "It's Been A While". I know it's about a drug-addicted man trying to make amends with a lover, but I apply it to where I'm at.

The lyrics speak to me and I love any song that has a swear word in it. It makes me feel like such a badass even though I'm just a mom from the burbs in Minnesota.

It has been a while since I could hold my head up high. And yes, I have stretched myself beyond my means. And hell yeah, it's been a while since I could say I wasn't addicted to my unholy thoughts.

But just one more peaceful day. And one more after that. And another one. Please let this recovery last.

I am not evil. I don't know what I'm fighting, but I do know I'm someone that is recovering from physical, mental and spiritual sickness. That's not demonic, that's life.

260

I still have a hard time choking down compliments or good things because I think, "Oh boy, if you really knew me, you might not be so good to me." I know there's a ton of work that still needs to be done, but I can't go there yet. It's too fresh and I'm still too vulnerable.

August 20, 2001 Night

Since sauna therapy didn't really go as planned, I tried running again. Those endorphins are supposed to be like little keys to relieving depression. I don't know if I'm depressed, but I do know I could be happier. So I ran today on lunch.

It was a bright, sunny day. It actually felt good. I was greeting other runners like I was one of them.

Then a BLACK CROW, a fucking BIRD, swooped down on my head and attacked my scalp. I was screaming and waving my arms, fighting off this heinous thing.

I was throwing punches toward the end just to make him pay with pain. I swear this was not a delusion. It really happened. My pulsating scalp tells me so. I'm certain it wanted to take me to its nest and feed me to its young.

I don't understand how this happens to me.

Why can't I seem to find my magical solution to relieving depression? I hear people all the time say, "Oh, I

Un-Perfect

just can't live without my morning run/yoga/sauna..."

Everyone seems to have a "thing", but I can't find a "thing" that works for me. And I really need something to pull out of this.

I suppose I could try yoga, but I heard there is a corpse pose, where you just lay there like you're dead. A corpse pose. When I 'm trying avoid suicidal thoughts.

DEREK

8/20/01

I would have paid big money to see that crow "attack" her head. It probably just flew a little close to her and she freaked. Kelly exaggerates everything.

But what if she seriously got hurt? I don't know what I would do.

She's my rock.

Or, at least she used to be.

August 21, 2001

Why am I a control freak? I'm starting to re-think my perspective on needing control. Isn't control what you exert when you're afraid things won't result in what you want?

I micro-manage everything because I'm afraid the outcome won't be what I want. It's rather narcissistic, actually. I want my way and I'm afraid I'm not going to get it if I let things flow.

I think there were some things that happened in my childhood that groomed me for craving control.

All my life I've been dodging bullets. Bad things have always missed me by an inch. Take for example, when I was five and my best friend Chrissy and I were at a park watching boys play hockey. A slap shot went bad and nailed Chrissy right in the mouth. There was blood everywhere, including on me. I had to walk her home in that state and when her mother opened the door, I was so scared. Her mother was hysterical, asking me what happened. I was five, so I was in no position to articulate what happened.

When her mother was screaming "WHAT HAPPENED!?" I internalized that to mean, "WHAT DID YOU DO!?" I blamed myself for the catastrophe that day. Maybe the puck was meant for me and I stood in the wrong place. Who knows, but her mother's hysterics were reason enough to believe that it was my fault. I'd never seen an adult so upset before.

Two years later, I was talking to my friend Allison from across the street. "Come on over!" I said, waving my arms. We were going to jump into leaf piles in my front yard. She took three steps and out of nowhere a car ran her over. I still hear the "thud" of that car hitting the body of a five-year-old girl when I think of this memory. Her mother heard the screeching brakes and ran

Un-Perfect

out into the street, cradling her scraped-up daughter begging me to answer, "WHAT HAPPENED!?"

I didn't know what happened. I was seven. She was coming over to jump in leaf piles with me and then she was going to the hospital. Neither of us saw the car coming. That's all my seven-year-old mind knew. Allison turned out to be fine and is thriving today, married with three children. Thank God. But I still feel responsible for that accident. If I didn't call her over, it wouldn't have happened.

Then when I was ten, my sister Kim and I were jumping on the trampoline with my uncle. We were teaching him how to do a back flip. He did what we told him to do, tuck in his knees and flip himself over to land on his feet. He broke his neck and had a seizure. The ambulance arrived and the same scenario of hysterics ensued. "WHAT HAPPENED!?" Or, as I heard it, *WHAT DID YOU DO?*

Once again, I didn't know what happened, I was ten. He did a back flip and it didn't work. That's all I knew.

But I knew something else: It was becoming clear to me that I was the source of all bad things. It's no wonder I like to control things. Look at all the shit that happened when I wasn't prepared for it. It seems to me that my childhood blueprint groomed me for some kind of breakdown. Children get hurt when I'm around them, then I had a child of my own. In my mind, she was bound to get hurt.

Motherhood cannot be controlled; it has to be held with fluidity. Mistakes will be made. Challenges will arise. It's not perfect and that's the beauty of it. I'm trying my hardest to believe this.

Perfection is not "mistake-less". Perfection is being here, having been created to learn and evolve. Perfection is who we already are and how we face challenges. Being called a Control Freak is not a compliment. It's being told that you're fearful and insecure.

At some point, I need to start holding life with an open palm. It's an old analogy: If you hold the soap too tight, it will slip away. If you hold it with an open palm, it will stay. Who wants to be bent over, ass naked, stumbling around the shower searching for the soap over and over again? Not me.

And it sucks every time it's dropped. I search around with shampoo stinging my eyes. It's painful. Life is painful when I try squeezing the living crap out of it.

August 21, 2002 Bedtime

I was an accidental magician tonight.

Derek and I went to a party tonight which should have been embarrassment-free. Should have, but wasn't.

I was talking and using my arms to punctuate a funny story and a sock came out of the wrist hole of my shirt. Why does this happen to me? Static must have clung the sock to the inside of my shirt and since I'm so expressive with my arms, it inched its way down and fell out at my wrist.

But you know what? It's funny. And I like funny. I just forgot it about it for a while.

August 22, 2001

The quirky thing about this whole mess is that at

Un-Perfect

the time, I didn't think I was missing anything. But now I feel like I woke up from being drunk on a neurosynaptic cluster-fuck.

I disengaged from life and it had the audacity to go on without me. I thought I was doing a great job living my life in those normal "in-betweens" when I wasn't dealing with psycho whiplashes.

But now that I'm better, I see that I missed everything. Sure, I saw my daughter laughing with my husband, but it was so far away. I didn't realize I was so tangled up in myself until I crawled out of my cave.

All my pre-occupations with myself glare in the bright light now. All that time I spent worrying, monitoring, recycling, and controlling myself. When a person implodes, you can only see the inside, nothing else.

The definition of implode is, "to burst or collapse inward." That is what happened to me. I collapsed into myself and had no time or energy for anyone else. Granted, they didn't know I wasn't giving them energy because I'm an extraordinary "fakeaholic." I can fake happy at any point in time.

When people around me were talking, sharing, and laughing with me, I wasn't emotionally available. I was obsessed with my health, my thoughts, and basically petrified of my own being. I lost opportunities to help friends in need. Yes, I would call and offer the right things, but it felt like a recording instead of sending my heart and truly being there for them.

Where is the Rewind button? Now that I'm back from my sabbatical in hell, I am ready to go back and re-experience birthday parties, happy hours and dates with the real me. The authentic me, not a copycat of someone else.

I want them back - all the conversations I missed when I was too busy mentally cutting out images and recycling them to concentrate on what people were saying. I'm ready to listen, cooperate, and respond, but the opportunity is gone. I can only listen to my friends and family going forward, making no reference to the past year. I don't know what happened to anyone else but me in the last year.

But maybe that's what survival mode is all about. Drawing into yourself, taking a look around, and getting rid of old rusty parts that don't work anymore. Taking time out to repair the wiring and hit the Reset button. And having the chance to recover and repair is giving me the reward of belief. I finally believe in myself.

I don't even care if I was adopted. But a part of me thinks I really was born into this family. I think I might belong with my parents and sisters. And for that matter, I think I belong with Derek and Parker.

And a very small part of me doesn't care if anyone is following me and planning to attack me. If someone wastes this much time following and tracking me, then so be it. I'm looking behind me a lot less these days.

August 23, 2001

I was (maybe still am) sick. I wouldn't harshly judge someone who has the flu, so why would I rake myself over the coals for being sick?

I did some research on lunch today and I think I found a home for my dis-ease, thought-slaughts, daymares, mental whiplash, and mind rapes.**

Un-Perfect

OCD. Who knew? I thought OCD was washing hands a million times or touching a doorknob a certain number of times. But that's not the case. It's so much more than that.

I feel NORMAL in a weird kind of way. I have a name. A thing. I finally have a "thing". Now I know what I'm fighting in the boxing ring.

Finally.

This is from the OCD Center of Los Angeles (reprinted in this book with permission of Tom Corboy, of the OCD Center of Los Angeles):

Symptoms

Perinatal / Postpartum OCD is a condition in which a woman's OCD symptoms begin or are exacerbated either during pregnancy or soon after giving birth. As in all cases of OCD, a woman with Perinatal / Postpartum OCD experiences obsessions **(repetitive, unwanted thoughts, ideas, or images),** and/or performs compulsions (repetitive behaviors) in an effort to avoid or decrease the anxiety created by these obsessions. In women with Perinatal / Postpartum OCD, **the focus of the obsessions is often on the fear of purposely or accidentally harming the newborn.**

Kelly Nordstrom

The OCD Center of Los Angeles offers the following brief questionnaire in an effort to help you get a better idea of whether or not you are exhibiting signs of Perinatal / Postpartum OCD. Simply check those items that apply to you, and email it to us using the simple form below.

While this questionnaire is not meant to replace a thorough evaluation, it may help in identifying traits of Perinatal / Postpartum OCD.

1. I worry excessively about purposely harming my child or others who I care about (i.e. suffocating my child, stabbing my husband).

Yes, Yes! I can't believe I'm not the only one! Oh thank God I'm not the only one! I'm not Satan, I'm just a person with postpartum OCD.

2. I frequently worry about accidentally harming my child or others I care about (i.e., accidentally poisoning my child, accidentally exposing my child to potentially dangerous household chemicals).

Yes, it's exhausting.

3. I excessively worry that I will be indirectly responsible for something bad occurring to my child (i.e., "I must ensure that my child is never exposed to certain things such as immunization shots, rare diseases, dangerous plants, etc., or else he/she could be seriously harmed and I would be responsible").

Yes.

4. I worry excessively that, if I don't perform certain superstitious behaviors, bad things will occur and it will be my fault (i.e. needing

Un-Perfect

to repeatedly tap on wood or say certain phrases in order to prevent my child from dying).

No. I don't think so? What about knotting plastic bags... that IS normal, right?

5. I prefer to minimize or avoid being alone with my child in order to avoid harming my child, or to avoid having thoughts about harming him/her.

No.

6. I avoid being around certain objects (i.e., knives, scissors, guns) in order to avoid harming my child, or having thoughts about harming him/her).

Yes.

7. I avoid driving with my child in order to ensure that I do not get into an auto accident with him/her.

I don't want her to ever get in a car. With anyone, including me.

Unfortunately, that's not reasonable.

8. I have great difficulty feeding my child because I am afraid I may poison or choke him/her.

No.

9. I often repeat routine, daily activities to ensure that I did not or will not expose my child to harm (putting away sharp objects, locking the house, turning off the stove).

Knotting plastic bags, wanting to put the knives in the cabinets, hiding baby oil...

10. I often repeat routine behaviors (e.g., getting dressed, turning off light switches, etc.) because I am concerned that I had a "bad" thought about my child when I initially performed that behavior.

Somewhere in here my bedtime routine comes into play, because I do it to relieve anxiety in case she wakes up in the middle of the night.

11. I excessively wash, shower, change my clothes, and/or use antibacterial wipes to ensure that I do not expose my child to germs, chemicals, insecticides, or other potentially dangerous things.

My house is a mess, but I do freak out about escalator belts, germ-infested indoor playgrounds, when she touches other kids, when she touches the grocery cart handle then sucks her on her fingers. I wish I could put "disinfectant mittens" on her hands every day...does such a thing exist?

12. I worry a great deal that my child has an illness, disease, or other medical condition, and that he/she will die if I fail to get appropriate treatment.

Hell's yeah. I worry she has cancer and I'm not catching the signs early enough.

13. I worry excessively that I don't really love my child.

No. I've loved Parker since the minute she was born.

I feel like I'm so over-protective of her that it

Backfired on me in the form of OCD.

Un-Perfect

14. I worry that I want to sexually molest my child.

    No.

15. I prefer to minimize or avoid being alone with my child in order to avoid having thoughts of sexually molesting him/her.

    No.

16. I prefer not to bathe my child or change his/her diapers because I am afraid I will sexually molest him/her, or that I will have thoughts about sexually molesting him/her.

    No.

17. I often recite prayers in an effort to rid myself of unwanted sexual thoughts or harming thoughts related to my child.

    No.

18. I repeatedly ask others for reassurance that I have not done something "wrong," "bad," harmful, or sexually inappropriate with my child.

    I like having reassurance that I'm a good mom – does that count?

19. I had some OCD prior to my pregnancy, but my obsessions and/or compulsions became more significantly more severe either during my pregnancy, or after I gave birth.

    Not sure?

20. I did not have any significant OCD features prior to my pregnancy, but developed obsessions and/or compulsions for the first time either during my pregnancy, or after I gave birth.

Yes, this feels right.

21. I am significantly distressed, anxious, and/or depressed about my obsessions and compulsions.

Hell to the yes on this one.

22. My obsessions and compulsions are interfering with my ability to care for my child.

Yes, I want to "wipe my mind's windshield clean"

so I can be authentic instead of feeling guilty

for my horrible, intrusive, obsessive thinking.

23. My obsessions and compulsions are interfering with my relationships and/or with my academic or professional functioning.

Yes. Try doing a budget sheet after obsessing about

an intrusive thought of a child being run over by a car.

24. I spend hours per day having obsessions and/or doing compulsions.

YES. YES. YES.

Treatment

Postpartum OCD is often treated with counseling and medication. Some women may be treated with anti-obsession medications. Other may receive the medication in combination with other forms of treatment or may not receive any medication at all.

Un-Perfect

One of the most effective CBT developments for the treatment of Perinatal / Postpartum OCD is Mindfulness-Based Cognitive-Behavioral Therapy. The primary goal of Mindfulness-Based CBT is to learn to non-judgmentally accept uncomfortable psychological experiences.

From a mindfulness perspective, much of our psychological distress is the result of trying to control and eliminate the discomfort of unwanted thoughts, feelings, sensations, and urges. In other words, our discomfort is not the problem – our attempt to control and eliminate our discomfort is the problem.

There it is. **Our attempt to control and eliminate our discomfort is the problem.**

I knew my control issues played into this shitstorm somehow. The beautiful thing I learned about OCD is that it has a lot of bark, but little or no bite. It's scary as hell, but since the victim is so scared of the thoughts, she rarely acts on them. It's relatively harmless compared to postpartum psychosis. And I say "relatively" because I'm sure shit has happened due to OCD. I'm lucky I'm not one of the statistics.

My question about OCD is this: Why the hell haven't I seen this questionnaire at my doctor's office? I kept getting the postpartum depression sheet jammed in my face at every visit, but I've never seen this sheet on OCD until I found it myself.

I found also this information on Postpartum Psychosis:

Symptoms:

With **postpartum psychosis** – a rare condition that typically develops within the first two weeks after delivery, signs and symptoms may include:

Confusion and disorientation

> **I named a chapter after confusion,**
>
> **but I don't think I was disoriented... was I?**

Hallucinations: Definition of hallucination: the apparent perception of sights, sounds, etc. that are not actually present.

> **I'm not sure on this one. My imagination was on over-drive, but I knew it was a thought in my head.**

Delusions: Definition of delusion: an erroneous belief that is held in the face of evidence to the contrary.

> **Believing I was Satan's daughter/I was adopted/I had a split personality. Delusions, yes or yes?**

Paranoia: Definition of paranoia: characterized by extreme irrational fear or distrust.

> **I thought my family had meetings to discuss my secret**
>
> **(The "Devil's daughter" thing).**
>
> **I was convinced that someone was stalking me in order to steal Parker.**
>
> **Wait, how do I know these are not real?**

Un-Perfect

Attempts to harm yourself or your baby:

No. Thank God. I was terrified of the fact that I COULD do harm, but never, ever attempted it - Just obsessed about the idea that I COULD.

I'm a little afraid to let go of the "paranoid delusions". And I put them in quotes in case *my* situation is real. What if I let my guard down, chalking it up to psychosis and then I get attacked? But what if they're NOT real and I'm wasting all this energy on nothing? What if the world isn't filled with people trying to kill me and steal my child? What if people are GOOD? But what if they're not? But what if they are? Again, I'm a dog chasing its tail. I do have an inkling of belief that I'm not the devil's daughter – I don't think that's true, but I'm not totally sure yet.

It's scary to try to convince myself that maybe the man that took our picture really was just wanting a picture of the Bjorn and selling it in his country. He seemed like a nice person. He didn't come within 20 feet of us. But what if I let my guard down and he DOES want to kill me and steal Parker? What if?!

The good news is this: I must be somewhat out of the hole in order to be aware of the condition.

The weird news is that it doesn't seem like psychosis hit me until after Parker was a year old.

I'm thinking perhaps I was psychotic because of the insane OCD. If the OCD wasn't there, I don't think I would have displayed psychotic bells and whistles. I was delusional because I couldn't explain the intrusive thoughts.

It's like I had an OCD sundae with a drizzle of depression and psychotic sprinkles.

** This date was changed for the sake of the book. The OCD screening was created in 1999, so it existed in August of 2001. However, I didn't "find a home for my kind of crazy" until December of 2009. I needed to somehow weave this extraordinary conclusion into the book because I wanted to share how I felt when I finally found and answered this screening. The rest of the book is a combination of my (semi) recovery in 2001 and my full recovery in 2009. While I pulled out of my suicidal state without ever realizing what I suffered from, I still wondered if I had schizophrenic tendencies - until I learned it was OCD. My full recovery did not happen until December 2009, when I finally realized that I suffered from postpartum OCD and worked with a therapist to learn tools to deal with it.

August 23, 2001 Night

Derek and I went out for dinner tonight and sat next to a group of geriatrics. One of the old guys got sick and started barfing. I was scared that he was going to die.

The restaurant staff was huddled around the old man with washrags and buckets, asking if he was okay. It was crazy.

Then Derek leaned across our table and said, "You know what I'm loving about this situation? The other grandpa that's still eating his dinner."

I looked over and he was right. The other old guy at the puking table was still shoveling salad into his mouth. I'm

*thinking there's an unwritten rule that once a person hits 80,
they're exempt from etiquette.*

*Man, did we have a good time laughing about it
tonight. I mean, the sick guy turned out to be okay and
everything, so it was fine to laugh about it. I love laughing
instead of worrying.*

August 24, 2001

*I'm not schizophrenic. I don't have a split
personality. I'm not the Devil's daughter. I simply have
postpartum OCD.*

*It's like there has been a smoky screen wedged
between Parker and I and it has been lifted. All this time
I've been working to crush through it, hoping she'll feel my
love despite this postpartum mess.*

*Without the overlay of OCD's intrusive images
projecting across my mind, I can see her, really see her
beautiful face. I've always known she was pure love, but to
be able to appreciate it with my entire soul is a new
experience.*

*Well, maybe not new, but renewed. As I felt in the
hospital when I first had her, my entire heart and soul wraps
around her.*

Kelly Nordstrom

Postpartum OCD, depression and psychosis are threaded into the fabric of my life now. The experience is transforming me into who I am and who I am going to be. Nothing has been wasted. It took each and every step to get to where I am now.

I am conquering what I consider to be a severe mental illness without medication. It's time to take a step back and appreciate how far I've come and give myself an Atta Girl.

Even on my "two-steps-back" days, I can be aware of the experience instead of sinking into it. I understand when it's a "two-steps-back" day and I'm entitled to have them. It's frustrating trying to beat your mind at a game you've never played. I've been known to cry over losing at Monopoly, so of course I'm entitled to some tears to wash out the intense irritation when I realize it's not gone.

I'm almost there and I feel good. I worry about sliding back into it, so each step forward is tentative. Like rock climbing. I grab the next rock, swallow my fear, and tentatively exhale thinking, "Okay, okay. Good. Today is good." That's what every day is like for me.

Or more precisely, every few hours. I'll make it through the entire morning without one intrusive thought and finally exhale. Then I'll do the gold swirling just in case. Then dinnertime will come and go. Exhale. I started doing the meditation stuff during the day because I don't have the luxury of saving it for night. Every tool needs to be immediate. I have my scraps of paper in my pocket, recycling my thinking, and meditation throughout the day. They have to be at my beck and call every minute because they are saving my life.

Do I still worry about what life is going to serve up? Absolutely.

Do I avoid things in life because of this fear? Absolutely not.

Un-Perfect

August 25, 2001

The word "survival" somehow sounds tragic to me. When I say I'm a survivor of postpartum OCD, depression and psychosis, it sounds tragic to me. I'm grateful my experience wasn't tragic. It could have been, but it wasn't. It wasn't, but it COULD have been tragic. I could obsess about it, but I won't. I can't.

I'm just grateful to be on my way out of this. I don't really know how it's happening - maybe it really is all my tools and meditating – I don't know. I don't have the luxury of looking back yet because the slope is too slippery. I just know I'm on my way out and I'm not going to have a tragic ending to all this.

Are there tragedies in this world? Yes. Loved ones die. People get sick. Accidents happen. Mental illness sets in. It happens all around us. It happens TO us. It happens.

I'm kind of challenging my own spirit here by trying to have another baby. It's like a test to see how far I've come. I feel like I'm daring postpartum to try and get me this time so I can prove to myself once and for all that I'm not susceptible to having it sink me again. I can't be looking over my shoulder and living in fear that it will come back. I need to know that it was a temporary thing that I've overcome and it won't get me again.

I don't want to wait four or five years and then have it come back. If it's going to come back, then let it be now so I can complete my family and get on with my life.

August 28, 2001

I don't want to die. I had a nightmare that it was my turn to die and it was decided that it was going to happen before the sun rose.

I was at peace with it, but then realized I didn't say goodbye to Parker, Derek, my parents, my sisters, all my friends. There wasn't enough time. I kept panicking, waiting for death to come, but it never did.

It took me a while to realize it was a dream. Not real. I'm going to live. This world is going to let me live.

August 31, 2001

Holy shit, I'm pregnant.

I'm shocked. Derek is shocked.

It's so weird how a person is forming in my body. There's so much going on in there and I have no control over any of it. I just have to trust that my body is

Un-Perfect

forming a brain. Not to mention hair follicles, toenails, teeth,
eyeballs and opposable thumbs.

How on earth does it happen? Two sets of DNA
zip up together to form a human being. I don't care what
anyone says, there is nothing more baffling than that. And it
happens without any instruction or direction from the outside
world. It blows my mind.

I've been given another chance to experience motherhood without the overlay of OCD, depression and psychosis. I find myself getting so frustrated when an intrusive thought does make its appearance. I'll usually say, "Go find another schmuck to do your dirty work and think your bad thoughts. You picked the wrong girl."

It's so frustrating to not have a handle on my thinking. I'm feeling so strong and courageous and then suddenly, "Oh, it's back again. Fuck."

But I *do* feel capable of having another baby. I have a handle on this and I'm excited about it. I'm a little leery about having psychosis reappear after I have the baby, but I refuse to have postpartum shit limit my dreams. Nothing will get in my way of hopes and dreams.

If anything, my experience is propelling me toward having another baby to prove that I can experience it all without the wicked postpartum overlay. I want to feel what it's like to hold my newborn and just let it flow, holding life with an open palm.

DEREK

9/1/01

Holy shit. Here we go again.

9/2/01 Sunday Muffins At Mom's

Mom and I had coffee at the counter this morning and I started slowly dripping out more details about my experience with postpartum OCD. I held my warm cup of coffee next to my face, breathing in the steamy swirls and said, "Mom, it was bad. I'm just now realizing how bad it was. I was suicidal for a while. And uh, I thought I was the devil's daughter. I was nuts, Mom."

If she was shocked, she didn't show it. She said, "Oh, I wish you would've told me, Kelly. You went through it alone when we were all right here. There's no reason for you to ever do anything alone, honey. Never."

I have tears in my eyes as I write this because there a well of compassion, love, and help waiting for me and I chose not to see it. People would have cared for me, but I chose to turn the other way. I would have

Un-Perfect

had a gentle hand on my shoulder when I cried on the bathroom floor all those years ago. But it happened the way it was supposed to happen, I guess. No regrets.

Mom leaned back and said, "You know, I wonder if that's not what Grandma had. My mother was in bed for months after having my brother. She would not get out of bed and was rather adamant about it. My sister basically raised him until my mother got out of bed. I wonder if she suffered alone too.

I was just a teenager at the time, so I didn't think anything of it. She just said she was sick and I never questioned it. But what was she sick *with*? No one knew and no one asked."

I wish I could ask Grandma why she was adamant about staying in bed for months all those years ago, but she's not here anymore. I want to ask her if her mind terrified her and the only way she knew how to keep everyone safe was to stay in bed until it passed.

Maybe it was depression. Maybe life folded in on her and she couldn't see a way out. We'll never know the details, but if I was a bettin' gal, I'd put all my money on postpartum depression, OCD and/or psychosis.

September 11, 2001

Grief and panic reverberated across the world like an emotional sonic boom. Attacks on U.S. soil today. Vibrations of sadness were felt across the world. A person can't help but mourn when something of this magnitude is released onto the planet.

Everyone looks emotionally naked and vulnerable. It's kind of beautiful when you see care in such raw form.

I always get this feeling when I go to a funeral. No one is wearing their ego cloak. People are incredibly authentic when they grieve and I think it's a beautiful thing to have the façade fall away. At funerals, we are surrounded by good people with big hearts. I can feel intense love and care as I sit in a pew at a funeral. Everyone there is connected by honoring one person. Everyone has the same goal of coming together, not only to honor the deceased person, but to sit with their own thoughts of what their legacy will be when they die.

It's a big question.

What do you stand for? What do you believe in? Do you inspire this world and the people in it or do you sit quietly mumbling about the unfairness of it all? Who ARE YOU?

Everyone is doing a little soul-searching now, with the understanding that it could be taken away at any given

Un-Perfect

second.

A lot of people know it all too well, sitting on their kitchen floor sobbing for the loss of their spouses, parents, children or friends. They sit in numbing denial, hoping it was a mistake and their loved one will walk through the door any minute.

But the sun will rise tomorrow without anyone turning the knob. "If only I did this, if only I said this, if only this happened..." If only war didn't exist. If only.

The world is quiet. It is so weird to look into the sky and not see one plane. Or hear them. We are all silent with our thoughts and grief. Perhaps something of this magnitude will unite people on earth. We will learn to care for others' spirits and well-being. We all share the common denominator of surviving tragedy. Together, we live and prosper.

September 12, 2001

People woke up this morning without their loved ones. Actually, I'm certain none of them slept, so instead of waking up, they simply got up. Off the floor or out of the chair they were sitting in all night, clinging to a soft blanket, feeling the sting in their hearts.

How do you breathe when your loved one doesn't?

Mothers are making toast for their children this morning and what will they say when the little ones ask, "Where's Daddy?" How does a person live with half of a heart? No matter what the age or relationship to you, when someone you love dies, it feels like they take a piece of your heart with them.

Sometimes, you didn't even know they had ownership of that corner of your heart until they're gone and you feel that pull and tug as they take it with them.

*Parker definitely takes up a ton of real estate in my heart. Despite my postpartum experience with her... scratch that, maybe because **of** my postpartum experience with her, I feel intense love for her.*

Like my heart is trying to catch up for lost time, so the faucet is turned all the way to the right. Letting all the love flow in. I'm grateful for my life and everything and everyone in it.

It's almost like I use this statement as a shield against bad things. See world? I'm grateful, I don't need a lesson to teach me gratitude, so leave me alone. Please don't target me for anymore of life's teachings right now. I'm just dusting off my knees from the last one.

But these people, they didn't invite this. No one

does. No one requests tragedy in their lives. Victims of 9/11 were grateful too, feeling so happy with their lives. It's just how the journey goes, I guess. I wish there was a better explanation for it.

What sucks is that we don't see what's coming. Life doesn't come equipped with headlights. All we can do is enjoy right now. Maybe that's exactly why life doesn't come with headlights – it forces us to enjoy the Now.

Tragedy struck, but it didn't hit me. Maybe I don't have a target on my back after all.

September 15, 2001

I think people muster up a little too much courage driving their cars. Maybe it's because they're contained in their own special little suit of armor. But the flipping off, nodding heads, shaking fists, and leaving notes on windshields is overkill.

I always seem to be the target even though I swear I'm not a bad or inconsiderate driver.

I have to drive Derek's truck this week because mine is getting fixed. It's a big manly truck. I can't park the thing to save my life. It's like driving a motor home. Anyway, I semi-parked at Target to grab the usual: toilet paper, birthday cards, and shampoo.

I got back to the monster truck to find a note under the windshield that read: "Nice park job. Maybe next time you could leave a can opener so I could get into my car. ASSHOLE."

Really? Is that necessary? I'm trying to enjoy the "Now", but it's a little difficult when I'm being called an asshole.

9/16/01 Sunday Muffins at Mom's

Sitting at the counter today surrounded by my husband, baby, parents, sisters, nieces, nephews and brothers-in-law was an incredible feeling. The old me wouldn't say anything mushy or sappy out loud, but there was something about today that unlocked my guards. I said out loud to everyone, "I'm just so thankful that we're all here, alive and good."

That's a stretch for me to say something like that to everyone, but I couldn't help it. I love each and every person that walked through that door today. It's an intense feeling of gratitude. My sisters married good men, my parents are healthy and smiling,

Un-Perfect

my daughter hugs and kisses me, my husband is amazing, my nieces and nephews are great kids.

Thank God, thank God, thank God.

I told them I was pregnant and the reactions ricocheted around the kitchen like a super ball. "Wait, what just happened? Who's pregnant?" One after another, "Wow! I didn't know you were even trying!" and "That's great you guys, you'll love having two."

I joked about Derek being a sharp shooter, which made him cringe and want to crawl into a hole. I don't know why I love embarrassing him so much in front of my family. Probably because it's so easy. But all jokes aside, they're happy for us and can't wait to meet the new addition in nine months. Nine months feels like forever.

September 17, 2001

It seems I have a postpartum hangover that will never recede.

I'm convinced that I will forever need to censor and police headlines, conversations, TV shows, books and photographs. My OCD just takes over and over and over again. Because that's what it is…obsessive.

I seem to have lost the "OFF" button on my brain. Just as an alcoholic cannot take that first sip, I cannot indulge in disturbing stories because I will pay the price.

I will ruminate and obsess, which seems to invite other disturbing thoughts and before I know it, I'm drunk on a seemingly psychotic binge. This requires me to "dry out" and get clean by meditating and recycling my thinking.

Just like an addict, I know it's wrong. I know it screws up my life. But the temptation is there. There are tragic stories everywhere. All I have to do is pick one, and then start drinking in all the gory details until my obsessive chops are satisfied.

It's like one evil thought attracts five more and those five attract five more. So it's important to recycle it out before it multiplies. It never reaches the severity of what it was a few months ago and I don't feel at risk of sliding into the crazy pool as I used to. It's more of a sensitivity that I have now to disturbing information.

But that's okay. If I'm left with some scars from defeating hell, so be it.

Since an alcoholic has a sponsor, I think a postpartum survivor could benefit from a sponsor as well. Someone that has been through the rocks and came out on the other side. Someone to give a person strength when they are running low. Anyone going through it needs to be reminded that they are indeed a good person, normal person.

Couldn't there be a type of Hazelden for people recovering from a postpartum shitstorm? Somewhere a person could stay and be safe and have

Un-Perfect

intense therapy and support? Maybe a massage or two? Meditation circles would be nice. Shouldn't there be a type of family counseling to prepare and educate them and teach them how to support their loved one? I'm thinking this place would have white, clean walls and for breakfast they can have English muffins, jelly side up every single morning.

September 18, 2001

I didn't order this. When I sat at the dinner table and put in my request for a baby, I didn't sign up for colic, postpartum OCD, depression, psychosis, delusions and hallucinations. I didn't even know this shit was on the menu.

I'm used to sitting at the table and banging my fork and knife up and down demanding my life to be in order. It didn't work this time. Why was this served to me? Why couldn't the mom sitting next to me at the restaurant get all of this crap? Then again, why NOT me?

Healing is a tough job and there is a reason for it. It rips a person apart and there is nothing to cling to but the raw bones of who you are.

I didn't get what I ordered, but I got what I needed. I think I'm a better, stronger person now.

When we're faced with a challenge, a lot of us think, "Why is this happening to ME?" I'm certainly doing that now.

Here's my shot at trying to uncover the lesson learned in what seems to be bullshit situations:

People laid off from work learn self-worth. They understand they are still loving, loyal, fun, and caring. A "non-paycheck" doesn't change any of those things. They are just as worthy on Monday as they were on Friday. Same person, same smile, different day. A job does not define who we are.

People recovering from depression learn compassion. Their hearts go out to people moving through their days wearing a heavy, sleepy, dark, coat and trying to smile over the numbness of it all. They reach out with complete vulnerability and say, "I've been there. What do you need from me?"

Marriages that survive affairs become stronger and more committed. A marriage is reborn. Love is injected into a relationship that was once on life support. The couple soars in security and strength.

In marriages torn apart, they learn to walk on their own two feet. They realize that another person cannot take their love, confidence, and esteem. Indeed, those things were *not* split 50/50 with their spouse. They get to keep them 100%.

People dealing with addictions learn self-control. They

Un-Perfect

walk through this world with non-judgment and acceptance. They understand that people struggle with things inside themselves that no one else can see.

People dealing with illness learn appreciation. They become stronger, even more grateful, and they love without abandon. When facing death, they learn to live. They teach the rest of us to stop and smell the fucking roses already. It takes 5 seconds, just do it.

People dealing with heartache and loss learn faith. Faith in the unknown, a place none of us can possibly grasp with our worldly hands. They move in this world with a little less to fear than the rest of us, because they survived what could be the worst fear of all: Losing a child, spouse, mother, father, sibling.

All the difficult lessons we learn, all the triumphs we celebrate... it's all here for us to experience. So when we say, "Why ME?" It's because we're here. We're here to have it all. And that means there is no filter to pick and choose. There is no lifting of the silver plate topper and saying, "Ah shit, I didn't order this, send it back."

We have no choice other than to grow, learn, teach, and shine.

Okay. Getting off my soapbox now.

September 19, 2001

What kind of mother has intrusive thoughts of harming people, including her daughter?

One that was physically, mentally, and spiritually sick.

A mother that is prepared to help other women move through this challenge.

A mother determined to revolutionize treatment and care for anyone having a difficult postpartum experience.

A mother who was petrified of any harm coming to her child; whose protection mode was on overdrive.

A mother that has learned to love, forgive, and be more compassionate than she ever thought possible.

A mother that has always loved her daughter, even when she shared her life with a terrifying condition.

Instead of writing out Notes Of Five, I write down one good thought now. I write it a few times and tuck it into my jacket pockets, jeans pockets, I post it on my bathroom mirror.

"You deserve good things. The universe stretches out its hands and gives you a gift. You are meant to have it and it is meant to stay. Treasure your gifts."

Un-Perfect

I do. I treasure Parker and the life and light she brings to me. She is pure love. Pure joy. I treasure Derek and his unshakeable love for me. I still haven't divulged my entire experience to him, but I will. When the time is right I will tell him everything.

I treasure my parents, sisters, their husbands, and nieces and nephews. I know they're there for me if I ever need support again. It's a slow process, but I'm learning how to tentatively receive good things into my heart, even though I still struggle with whether or not I deserve them.

I think survival means having the opportunity to crack myself open and soar a little higher. It demands transformation into a better person.

Survivors of anything are courageous, compassionate and loving. They have an appreciation for life and how it flows. They know it's not all perfect and peaceful. There are rocks and waterfalls, but they no longer live in fear of them. They honor the flow. That's what a survivor is to me.

September 21, 2001

I wasn't feeling well, so the doctor requested an ultrasound for me. I didn't have time to call Derek and tell him the doctor was concerned. I just floated forward into the ultrasound room.

I was so nervous, I started cracking jokes, trying to laugh my way to a healthy baby. My philosophy is that if the technician likes me and thinks I'm a good person, then the outcome will be good. Good attracts good.

But it didn't work. The ultrasound technician had

no bedside manner at all. She didn't even laugh at my jokes. She pointed to the screen and said, "You have nothing viable here."

She walked out and I was alone. Not even a baby in my belly to keep me company.

You have nothing viable here.

While this news feels like a serrated knife on my soul, I know what it feels like to have nothing viable. The definition of viable is "the ability to live or succeed." I have endured the feelings of not having the ability to live or succeed, and I overcame it. This is just a bump in the road. Life flows and I need to let it do its thing. My life is not going to end because of a miscarriage. Parker's life is not going to end because of it. And Derek will be home to hug me when I get there.

I'm worried about my hormones. They are going to crash and make me pay the price for trying to grab my dream too early. I've come so far with my disease, I hope this crash doesn't upset my progress.

I started in on some major cheek-biting, cutting rows on both sides of my cheeks. They're so sore, it's actually painful to speak. But in a crazy way, it feels good and I can't help it. It's my compulsion and I can't *not* do it in times like these.

You have nothing viable here.

There was a time when I believed that statement. My life was hopeless and filled with excruciating, horrific slideshows. But not anymore. I'm surrounded by beautiful life even though I don't currently have one tucked into my belly. But it will happen. He or she is waiting with wings right now and will

Un-Perfect

come when the time is right.

It's difficult for my heart to take this in, but I'm not going to protect myself and pretend it's perfectly fine. I will cry on Derek's shoulder when I get home.

You have nothing viable here.

While this is sad and painful, it won't knock me down. Not back to that place I was a few months ago. I won't slide back to that dark place because something didn't go my way. I will watch myself carefully and get a lot of rest, drink gallons of water, meditate, scratch out affirmations on scraps of paper and recycle my thoughts if my mind starts torturing my well being.

I have tools to maintain a great life. I have people that love me and will support me if I need a gentle place to fall. Damn, it feels good to be surrounded by people that love and care for me.

You have nothing viable here.

Yes I do. I have a beautiful life. How dare anyone try to tell me otherwise.

I believe in life and everything it has to offer. I float along the river over the sharp rocks, down the falls and into the peaceful flow. I'd do it again and again and again.

I do have something viable here.

I have love, life, belief, strength, courage, and support.

Not only have I made it, I made it better.

EPILOGUE

Love yourself.

How can you receive love
if you don't recognize it?

Un-Perfect

I was pregnant three weeks later and had our daughter Paige Judith on June 27, 2002. I enjoyed the ups and downs of having a toddler and newborn without any kind of depression or psychosis.

Derek was adamant about making me rest. I drank water and meditated often. I posted notes of encouragement on the bathroom mirror and on the fridge. The OCD still sticks with me a bit, but I'm learning good tools to cope. I have experienced nothing as severe as what I survived during that postpartum period after my first daughter.

Physically, my thyroid was tested on 9/24/01 and it came back normal. I don't know where this fits into the puzzle, but I believe it is a contributor. I have it tested twice a year to keep close tabs on it. While it seems volatile, it has never sunk or soared out of normal range again.

It's been eight years since my experience with postpartum OCD, depression and psychosis. Even now, it's still hard to believe it happened.

As hard as I tried to forgive and trust myself, I couldn't do it alone. I found a therapist (a.k.a. "The Couch") to help me. I didn't realize how little trust I had in myself until we started moving through our sessions together. Those were some bumpy roads, but all worth it.

Why do people think that seeing a therapist makes them crazy? If you want to hit the Reset Button on your life, then isn't it crazy *not* to see one? It's ironic that when I actually was crazy, I was considered fine because I wasn't seeing a therapist. But when people learned I was seeing one, they considered me nuts. Now *that's* crazy to me.

I finally got to the bottom of my cheek-biting. It's like cutting, a term I was not familiar with until The Couch told me about it. I was shocked to realize it's a serious psychological disorder – OCD can have a trait of cutting. Didn't know that. The Couch explained to me that cheek-biting was a way of externalizing emotional pain into physical pain, to control and localize it. It also released endorphins to numb the inflicted site, the same goodies released when we exercise. I created physical pain, then fixed it, instead of dealing with my emotions. I worked so hard at being stoic that I'd defer to physical pain instead of allowing myself to feel emotion.

I'm happy to report that my cheeks are healthy and good.

I also sleep peacefully every night without sleeping pills. Just like a big girl, I sleep through the night. Amazing.

When I say I recovered without medication or therapy, I mean that I only brought myself to a level of pure survival - I simply kept my heart beating. I did not fully recover until December of 2009. At that time I had been seeing a therapist for two years and that is when I discovered the perinatal/postpartum OCD screening. What a relief to finally let go of the confusion and understand exactly what happened to me. I used to think I didn't the label, but the label is knowledge. The label is a little door to understanding a new world of information needed to live the highest potential. No one should live in fear and confusion. It sucks.

I stand firm and censor information that surrounds and touches me. I'm an obsessive person with intrusive thoughts. It's nothing to be afraid of, it's just a fact. But I still take great care with what I read, hear and watch. People know this about me now and I really don't care if they judge me for it. Surprisingly, they don't. Instead, I feel closer to friends and family because they truly love and accept me for who I am. I'm not trying to be anyone else, I'm just me. I'm quirky. They seem to like the quirk. :)

As I write the Epilogue, my husband, parents, in-laws, and sisters are reading my unfinished, raw manuscript. This is the first time any of them are learning about the severity of what I experienced. Writing is the only way I could get it all out and share my heart and soul. If I could only bring two things to a deserted island, it would be journal and pen. Screw food, I need to write.

Un-Perfect

My sister Kari explained that she loves me unconditionally and I've always been a great mom, I just forgot for a while.

My mother is struggling with guilt for not being there for me during my struggle, but is proud of each and every word I've written. I have to remind her that it's impossible to help someone when they keep it a secret.

My sister Kim sees it as a gift that allows me to be there for other women in this world going through the same experience. They won't feel alone, like I did.

My dad just hugs me and calls me "Sweetieheart."

My in-laws struggle with guilt for not helping, but as I reminded my mother, a person can't help if they don't know.

Derek's perspective is written below in his final entry in this book.

This book has been healing for both of us, propelling us to talk about the experience. He, like my mom, is dealing with his own guilt for not being there for me. I remind him that it's impossible to help someone when they protect their secret as fiercely as I did.

Heal yourself, heal the world.

April 26, 2010

My 40th birthday! Once again, I feel special all day. Derek and I went out for a glass of wine to toast forty years. Parker and Paige asked the usual question over breakfast, "If you could be any age, what would it be?"

My answer is the same as it was last year: "Now. Now is where I always want to be. Every day I learn something new about myself, others, and this world. It took

*each and every day to get here, so I would never want to go
back."*

*They didn't believe me. They looked at each other
over their bowls of Lucky Charms. Paige said, "Are you sure
you don't want to be seven like me?"*

*I leaned on my elbows across the kitchen counter and
tucked her hands in mine and said, "Paige, if I met you when
I was seven, I bet we'd be best friends. But I met you as your
mother and if I turned back the clock, I wouldn't be your
mom. And I love, love, love being your mom. I like how
everything turned out. Do you?"*

She said, "Yeah, I like you for my mom."

*Parker, who is nine years old now, laughed and
said, "Dude, I feel so lucky to have you for my mom." She
calls me dude. It's a phase. At least I think it is.*

*We had cake at Mom's house last night and as I
blew out the candles, I closed my eyes and wished, "I wish for
my life to continue just like it is." We took a picture and
dad yelled, "Kelly's a DORK!"*

Some things never change. I like that.

Un-Perfect

"Celebration"

August, 2002. Celebrating Dad and Jake's birthday.

From the look on his face, we can assume my dad made his usual smartass comment before the picture was snapped.

Left to right (bottom): Derek, Holly, Jake, Ethan, Hanna, Parker

Left to right (top): Dad, Mom, Corey, Dennis, Kim, Pete, Paige, Me, Kari.

When this picture was taken I still didn't know what I suffered from when Parker was a baby. As much as I tried to soothe the fear, I still worried that I was schizophrenic and that it would come back some day and terrify me all over again. I feared that the symptoms simply went "underground," but they were still there, threatening to come back with a vengeance. I always worried it would come back.

Seven years later, I would FINALLY be completely healed and at peace with my postpartum experience. Finally. Peace at last.

10/6/09 PARKER SUE (9 ½ years old)

Love isn't something you earn, it's something you treasure.

DEREK

10/6/09

Kelly sent her manuscript to me. I cried and laughed and cried. I wasn't prepared for any of that. I'm sorry. For everything.

We've been talking about her postpartum stuff, but seeing it on paper is powerful. I'm learning the heartbreaking details and excruciating memories while reading this book. Sometimes I'll peek over in bed while she writes and I'll read a few sentences and think, "Holy shit, seriously?"

The word, "shock" feels like an understatement. I had no idea she went through all of this. Alone. She went through it all alone when I was sitting right next to her eating dinner, just the three of us. When we went on dates. When I joked with her about things. All that time she smiled her way through that sickening postpartum shit.

And I didn't know it.

I had no idea my wife sat crumpled on the floor of our bathroom crying, considering suicide. I had no idea that while I hugged her, she was "recycling" intrusive thoughts of gory, bloody death. It makes me cringe thinking about it. I still don't understand how a person can hate a certain thought, but think it anyway. But then again, I don't have OCD. I'm not wired like that.

But what would I have done back then?

I was a different person too. I was young - and if I'm being honest, I didn't know how to handle big things like that. A part of me thinks I denied knowing anything because I didn't know what to do.

It's heartbreaking to read it now, eight years after it happened. I don't know how I would've reacted if she told me when it was happening. I know I would've been afraid for everyone's lives, including Kelly's. I know I would have felt hopeless and frustrated, trying to fix it within a day. I would have wanted my wife back and wouldn't know when that would have been. I would have worried that she would never be the same again.

I'd love to say that I would have been strong, but honestly, I would've been a frustrated, frantic mess. I'm not proud of it, I'm just being honest.

Her postpartum experience happened the way it

Un-Perfect

happened. There's no changing it. I can't go back and make myself an "un-crappy" husband that didn't know his wife was hurting. I just have to move forward supporting her and letting her know that I'm strong enough to handle anything life throws at her.

Our family is a team. Never should any of us suffer alone. Ever.

That's what life is. Being a part of each other's lives; supporting, encouraging, listening, and loving.

Right Kel?

June 6, 2009

Right.

DEREK

10/6/09

I thought I'd let you have the last word since it's your book. Did you like that? I love you.

June, 10, 2009

Yes, I like that. I love you too, sweets. Now, sshhh, quiet. The book is done.

Kelly Nordstrom

"Joy and Peace"

Safe, loved, and surrounded by my favorite people (and dog) in the world: Derek, Parker, Paige and Rocket.

Un-Perfect

"Love and Forgiveness"

I love this little girl with all my heart.

I hope she loves and forgives me even though I'm

"Un-Perfect."

Resources

Postpartum Support International

Everything postpartum is found here. Amazing group of people.

1.800.944.4PPD

www.postpartum.net

Postpartum OCD

Tom Corboy is the founder of this center.

He created the OCD test I took – Thank God for Tom!

310.335.5443

www.ocdla.com

Postpartum online support group

Being a part of community is so important. Please don't suffer alone like I did.

www.ppdsupportpage.com

Un-Perfect

Support for fathers

Husbands may feel helpless and confused. Give this site a shot. It's cool.

www.postpartumdads.org

Postpartum Psychosis

Listing PSI again so people know to go here to get informed

and connected with the right help.

www.postpartum.net

Another option: Local hospital. No messin' around with this condition.

Understanding Postpartum Psychosis: A Temporary Madness

Author, Teresa Twomey. PSI Co-coordinator for Connecticut.

There is a secret.

1 in 8 women suffer from
postpartum depression.

Please don't keep it a secret.

By sharing your story with others
and getting help, you can be
the light to help show the way.

Heal yourself, heal the world.

Empowered Self-Publishing for an Enlightened New World

Indigo Heart Publishing helps you publish your book in the way that works best for you. We offer coaching to help you move from "Brainstorm to Best Seller" in six months or less. We custom create a publishing, coaching and marketing program that works for you and your budget.

Get Your Free Gift!

Please visit www.indigoheartpublishing.com and receive your free "From Brainstorm to Bestseller" audio course and learn how you can write a book in seven days or less.

The Indigo Heart Publishing website is a valuable resource for new information that can help you promote your books and keep you up to date on marketing news and trends.

We are always on the lookout for new promotion ideas and leading-edge writers. We welcome the chance to talk to you and see how we can help you become a published author so that you can leverage your time, increase your impact and your profit.

To see other titles published by Indigo Heart Publishing and to learn more about how you can become a published author, please visit our website at www.indigoheartpublishing.com.

www.indigoheartpublishing.com

Breinigsville, PA USA
24 August 2010
244193BV00002B/2/P